T0317591

Additional praise for

Win/Loss Reviews: A New Knowledge Model for Competitive Intelligence

"Gaining actionable and continuous competitive insights from win/loss analysis is key to developing insightful assessments of a company's strategic opportunities. This is the first book dedicated to providing a complete framework for win/loss reviews, with the added bonus of being written from the practitioner's perspective. It should be a part of any serious competitive intelligence library."

—Ken Garrison, CEO, Strategic and Competitive Intelligence Professionals (SCIP)

"Suddenly the lights came on! In *Win/Loss Reviews*, Rick manages to integrate sales and CI practitioner perspectives in such a complementary manner that this easy-to-read text expertly combines theory and practical execution for a step change in both sales and competitive performance."

—Andrew Beurschgens, Head, Market and Competitive Intelligence, Everything Everywhere Ltd.

"Winning in sales is all about taking the right action in support of the right opportunity at the right time. *Win/Loss Reviews* provides an effective method to illuminate these critical decisions in real time! No one should enter the competitive sales arena without this essential discipline."

—Paul H. Elliott, PhD, President, Exemplary Performance

"The ability to get to the 'why' around opportunity outcomes is critical to any organization that is seeking to learn from their past and present deals in order to impact future performance. In *Win/Loss Reviews* Rick creates an effective and compelling method to bridge information and feedback flow between sales and marketing and gives empirical evidence upon which to make sound business decisions. This methodology should be the cornerstone for any organization willing to look in the mirror, face truths, and promote the proliferation of knowledge."

—Bill Gang, Senior Sales Manager (Pharmaceutical),
Novo Nordisk

"This is a thought-provoking insight that provides us with a major weapon that any sales-oriented organization ought to have in its arsenal. *Win/Loss Reviews* is one of the best ideas I have come across in sales management in my 25-year consulting career. It provides a solid basis for a practical solution to overcoming the all-too-customary field argument that deals are only lost because of price."

—Barry I. Deutsch, Chief Consultant (Finance Industry),
Kotler Marketing Group

WIN/LOSS REVIEWS

A New Knowledge Model for Competitive Intelligence

RICK MARCET

WILEY

John Wiley & Sons, Inc.

Published by John Wiley & Sons, Inc., Hoboken, New Jersey.
Published simultaneously in Canada.

For general information on our other products and services or for technical support, please contact our Customer Care Department within the United States at (800) 762-2974, outside the United States at (317) 572-3993 or fax (317) 572-4002.

Wiley also publishes its books in a variety of electronic formats. Some content that appears in print may not be available in electronic books. For more information about Wiley products, visit our web site at www.wiley.com.

Library of Congress Cataloging-in-Publication Data:

Marcet, Rick.
    Win/loss reviews : a new knowledge model for competitive intelligence / Rick Marcet.
        p. cm.—(The executive leadership series)
    Includes index.
    ISBN 978-1-118-00741-9 (hardback); ISBN 978-1-118-10258-9 (ebk); ISBN 978-1-118-10259-6 (ebk); ISBN 978-1-118-10260-2 (ebk)
        1. Marketing—Evaluation. 2. Business intelligence. 3. Strategic planning. 4. Competition. I. Title.
    HF5415.13.M3437 2011
    658.4'038—dc22   2011012028

10 9 8 7 6 5 4 3 2 1

ABOUT THE EXECUTIVE LEADERSHIP SERIES

The Microsoft Executive Leadership Series is pleased to present independent perspectives from some of today's leading thinkers on the ways that IT innovations are transforming how organizations operate and how people work. The role of information technology in business, society, and our lives continues to increase, creating new challenges and opportunities for organizations of all types. The titles in this series are aimed at business leaders, policymakers, and anyone interested in the larger strategic questions that arise from the convergence of people, communication media, business process, and software.

Microsoft is supporting this series to promote richer discussions around technology and business issues. We hope that each title in the series contributes to a greater understanding of the complex uncertainties facing organizations operating in a fast-changing and deeply connected new world of work, and is useful in the internal dialogues that every business conducts as it plans for the future. It remains our privilege and our commitment to be part of those conversations.

Titles in the Executive Leadership Series:

*For my lovely wife, Lisa, and my
beautiful daughters, Michelle and Christine.*

CONTENTS

PREFACE

Globally successful organizations recognize that, indeed, only one asset grows more valuable as it is used—the knowledge skills of people. Unlike machinery that gradually wears out, materials that become depleted, patents and copyrights that grow obsolete, and trademarks that lose their ability to comfort, the knowledge and insights that come from the learning of employees actually increase in value when used and practiced.

—M. J. Margquardt, *The Global Advantage*[1]

This book is about tapping into one of the most underutilized sources of business intelligence—the collective knowledge to be gained from reviewing the opportunities that have reached the final decision stage of your sales processes. Simply put, these are opportunities that an organization has won or lost. It is also about the least leveraged creators of this knowledge: the *front-line sellers*. And it's about how technology and social media are enabling actionable intelligence to proliferate on many devices and form factors and across a broad set of stakeholders.

Having started my early business career in marketing for high-tech industries, I was eventually lured into the sales profession by the excitement I experienced in closing a deal with a customer. As a product manager for a midsize high-tech company, I frequently assisted our global sales teams by joining them on their sales calls, delivered several in-depth technical presentations, and helped them answer a lot of technical questions about their customers. Our customers' executives often wanted to get a sense of the product road map and how future releases would help support their vision and strategic initiatives. In most cases, however, I was called in to support our products against an incumbent competitor, or when we were about to lose our own incumbent position to a competitor. During the hundreds of sales calls I supported, I took copious notes about what the customers were saying about their needs, the tactics they were using, and anything said about our competitors. And when we won or lost the deal, I would debrief the account manager to see whether I could gain additional information that I had not previously captured.

This information started growing into a massive library of notes that I was able to reference in all calls that I supported. More importantly for me as a product manager, I was collecting valuable customer feedback during customer sales calls and from the sales teams. I took this information straight to our product development teams. After all, my job was to specify what we needed to produce in order to grow and remain competitive.

With so much exposure to selling with some brilliant sales professionals, and often being an integral part of helping sales teams close deals, I thought that sales was something I could do. The customer interactions were invigorating and each engagement was different. So when a sales position opened up, I jumped at the opportunity. As I already had a great information knowledge base to work from and reference, I considered myself quite successful even as a rookie account manager. Not only did I acquire great selling skills by observing and learning from lifelong sales professionals, I had amassed a comprehensive library of sales insights based on direct customer and sales team interactions. As my career in sales and sales management progressed, I continued to refine the process of collecting these valuable insights for future use against active opportunities, shared them with my team and among my peers, and created a collaborative bridge with the product development and marketing teams.

I didn't have a name for it at the time, but the early method created for capturing product and competitive insights from these sales interactions was the beginning of a *win/loss review framework*. The early experiences from this discipline actually form the practical and theoretical foundations of this book. Much of this is reflected in the institutionalized and global win/loss review program used today at Microsoft.

Perhaps it was fortuitous that I was coming into an organization like Microsoft, which embraced the concept of improvement through continuous learning, feedback, and knowledge sharing. Indeed, the culture of self-critiquing is deep-rooted in Microsoft's product development history. So, perhaps the success of the win/loss review program driven by the sales teams isn't so unusual, at least not for Microsoft. In their landmark book, *Microsoft Secrets*, Cusumano and Selby dedicate an entire chapter to the culture of learning at Microsoft, albeit largely through the eyes of the early product development teams.[2]

Similar to how the developers learned through rigorous post-mortems of every product test, release, and version, every business opportunity offers insights that can be leveraged as reference and applied toward future opportunities. Some insights are general and can be broadly applied; others are very specific to the nature of the opportunity. Combined, the collection of insights can point to heretofore unseen strategic opportunities, expose product or service deficiencies, and uncover otherwise-unknown competitive strengths that can be exploited as well as risks to be mitigated.

There is yet another dynamic that could not have been foreseen: As the information becomes widely available to a broad stakeholder audience, the buzz begins to create additional demand for broader integration, influencing and accelerating the normalization of data taxonomies and promoting the concept of "one version of the truth."

For your existing customers and prospects, it means receiving proposals of higher quality and competitive differentiation, optimized and enriched with the collective knowledge of prior experiences. And since customers are looking for their business partners and suppliers to bring them new and innovative ideas to grow their business versus proposed solutions that address only existing business challenges, win/loss reviews form a rich library of innovative ideas and solutions that can be referenced and reused.

Understanding the potential impact of conducting win/loss reviews and knowing how to surface and apply the insights gained requires a healthy balance of both art and science. Planned properly, a win/loss review process will gain broad internal stakeholder support and, more importantly, eager and willful participation by the sales force to reflect and share their knowledge in a meaningful way. In the end, the value gained will far outweigh the relatively small investment to aggregate these valuable pieces of *micro-intelligence* into a brilliant and insightful assessment of your own place in the competitive landscape. The smart business in the digital age will harness the power of connected systems and knowledge, and will no longer ask *if* but *when* it will implement such a powerful and indispensible discipline.

Finally, although many consider that the activity of reviewing opportunities that have been won or lost should be a "sales basic," it is far from being a naturally occurring activity in the course of the sales cycle—it is even absent in most sales models. Hence, this book recognizes win/loss reviews as an advanced sales skill and assumes that the sales or sales management professionals who are reading it consider themselves highly skilled in the sales profession.

More specifically, this book assumes that the sellers have a command of their customers' or prospects' needs and decision criteria, understand their competitive environment, and are disciplined in whatever sales model and tools they employ. This book does not cover basic sales skills such as securing appointments with decision makers, delivering sales presentations, or writing effective proposals—these truly are the basics that any high-performing sales professional should already have mastered.

Whether you are a seller looking to unearth those nuggets of information that will give you an edge over your competitor's offerings, a product manager looking for feedback on product positioning, or an executive planning the next strategic competitive play, there is no richer or more real-time data set to inform your strategy than that which is garnered from the opportunities that have exited your sales opportunity pipeline.

NOTES

1. M. J. Margquardt, *The Global Advantage: How World-Class Organizations Improve Performance through Globalization* (Houston: Gulf Publishing Company, 2005), p. 193.
2. M. Cusumano and R. Selby, *Microsoft Secrets: How the World's Most Powerful Software Company Creates Technology, Shapes Markets, and Manages People* (New York: Touchstone, 1995).

ACKNOWLEDGMENTS

In many ways, the inspiration for writing this book came from the realization that the sales professionals with whom I work are becoming increasingly open and disarmingly self-critical in their quest to learn more from their business outcomes and from peer experiences. So, my first expression of gratitude and thanks goes to professional salespeople worldwide, and especially to those at Microsoft who have contributed so much to this body of knowledge.

The person who most influenced my early career transition into the sales profession with his inspiring sales calls, charisma, and passion for selling is Pat Shanahan, formerly of Equitrac Corporation. Pat is the salesperson whom I still consider my personal standard bearer in the sales profession.

The spark for actually putting everything down on paper and sharing this knowledge for the benefit of others came from fellow author Mark Mueller-Eberstein, author of *Agility*, a business title published through John Wiley & Sons under the Microsoft

Executive Leadership Series. As this was my first business title, I had a lot to learn, and I am grateful for the patience and expert guidance afforded by Sheck Cho, my executive editor, and Laura Cherkas, my production editor, both at John Wiley & Sons. Helping me navigate through the early process was Jan Shanahan from Wild Sky Industries.

The opportunity to direct the global World Class Selling program, of which the win/loss review process is a core element, was an honor afforded me by Gerri Elliott, a corporate vice president at Microsoft and the first sponsor of the win/loss review program. For supporting the broad institutional rollout and ongoing sponsorship, I've relied very much on the feedback and advocacy provided by Austen Mulinder, Corporate Vice President, Worldwide Communications Sector, and Susan Hauser, Vice President, Worldwide Industry and Global Accounts, and by my managers, Rose Gyotoku and John Jester, who are the best program champions one could ever ask for.

When it comes to having landed the win/loss review program internally, I owe special thanks to David Vander and Martina Milligan of our Worldwide Sales Excellence team, whose leadership made this part of our daily sales rhythm. Early pilots and global advocacy with field competitive intelligence teams were supported by Michael Gorriarán from CMSG; thanks to Andy Erlandson, Jules Dickerson, Suzanne Hall, and Carmen Rodero-Scardelis from our competitive escalation team in CATM for the early support and integration with our competitive escalation processes.

Of course, this book also draws on the learnings gained from implementing and managing the global win/loss review process itself. For this I thank my lead consultant and project manager, Steve Puchala, from The Grasp Group. There were so many leading-edge and innovative technologies that made the information and insights a pleasure to explore and discover. Matt Jubelirer at Microsoft Live Labs gave us early support and encouragement for using Pivot (featured in a TED conference presentation by Gary Flake) for the remarkable visualization, and Michael Brophy and his team at Sysgain Inc. for their expertise in system integration, user interface, and mobile app development skills. Luke Hartsock and his team at Decisive Data designed additional innovative BI visualizations with Silverlight, which made the insights available to a broad group of stakeholders.

Reflecting a true blend of art and science, the mentoring I received from Six Sigma Master Black Belts Sabra Schriner and David Suhrie brought process chaos into order. The benefits went way beyond process improvement, but extended well into providing insights for the entire program.

During the course of research for the win/loss review program over the years, I've been fortunate to have learned from likeminded professionals involved in sales and sales operations from several other high-tech companies. There are bits of insights shared from companies such as IBM, AT&T, Cisco, Citrix, HP, SAP, and various consulting firms that specialize in competitive intelligence. For his mentoring and and for helping me see the bigger picture across industries, I thank Nick Ward, president and CEO of Supply Market Intelligence & Integration Inc. and a board member at Strategic Accounts Management Association (SAMA).

I learned so much and gained a great deal of perspective from Ellen Naylor, CEO and chief blogger at Cooperative Intelligence Source and a former Strategic and Competitive Intelligence Professionals (SCIP) board member; she is one of the most prolific and respected subject matter experts on competitive intelligence and on the topic of win/loss reviews.

Thanks to Brian Dietmeyer, president of Think! Inc., a negotiations consultancy, for his contributions to this book and early influences on the win/loss review process design. I'd be remiss if I didn't recognize the tremendous influence on the success of the win/loss review program of having participated in the

High Performance Leadership workshop at IMD in Lausanne, Switzerland. It was taught by the distinguished Dr. George Kohlrieser, author of the international bestseller, *Hostage at the Table: How Leaders Can Overcome Conflict, Influence Others, and Raise Performance.*

Much of this book deals with the rise of social media and their influence on our personal and professional culture. Paolo Tosolini, a social media expert and Web 2.0 consultant, provided great insights and advice for touching new audiences and building awareness across the Web.

I've always been the curious and inquisitive sort, but the one who first taught and inspired me to organize my thoughts and analyze the facts through numbers was my father, Carlos E. Marcet, P.E. The knowledge and discipline he gave me is reflected throughout this book. Thanks, Dad!

Finally, this book could not have been written without the support and encouragement of my wife, Lisa, and my two daughters, Michelle and Christine. Ladies, I promise to make up for the precious time you so generously gave me to complete this book!

CHAPTER 1

INTRODUCTION

The beginning of wisdom is to call things by their right names.

—Proverb

It's an interesting paradox—you expect your sales teams around the world to know exactly when they will close their deals, which, when combined and analyzed, drive your forecasts and ultimately your guidance to investors. But you don't really know *why* you are winning and losing deals. And you are expected to make strategic decisions that do not accurately factor in what the sales teams are experiencing on a day-to-day basis.

Or perhaps you're a seller involved in a complex competitive deal trying to get the latest tactical information that will help you win. Your marketing team is telling you to repeat the elevator pitches from their polished slide deck, but they are not talking to you or your specific sales situation. You desperately look for case studies or subject matter experts, but you need the information now or it's over.

Knowing why a company wins or loses is important to improving business performance as well as the company's ability to predict its business outcomes. Driving business performance beyond organic growth takes a combination of innovation, intelligence, customer alignment, and repeatable strategies that drive predictable and successful outcomes. Yet, today, it is estimated that fewer than 10% of the managed opportunities that are won or lost in an organization are reviewed with any amount of rigor. This can expose companies to growing competitive threats found in all areas of their business.

There are many factors that affect whether an opportunity is won or lost. When combined and analyzed, these factors turn into valuable insights that can point to new strategic opportunities, expose potential product or service deficiencies, and uncover otherwise-unknown competitive strengths and weaknesses. Getting to those insights requires that companies are thoughtful about documenting their approaches and self-critical when there is an opportunity for learning.

If asked why you are winning or losing in any particular sales scenario, are you able to provide an accurate and confident reply? In sales, we often rely on the talents of the sales teams to deliver the results, yet we're not really sure of the impact the sales teams have on the outcomes. We must believe that sellers are a critical part of this process, enough so that we spend billions of your hard-earned currency each year training them, assuming that the theory they learned in the classroom will immediately translate into higher performance.

Yet, there are so many other factors apart from sales team effectiveness that contribute to sales performance that are often overlooked. Some of these factors relate directly to the skills of the sales team; others include product, brand perception, services, intermediaries or partner channels, and so on. There is often a strong tendency to look closer at the factors the closer they are within our control, and assume there is causal correlation between these and our performance. This creates fertile ground for tactical and strategic blind spots, which increase performance risks.

The importance of establishing strong and trusted personal relationships is well documented and widely accepted in the sales profession as *the* primary variable within our control. It is often said that people buy from people they know and trust. There are several variations of this business axiom, but the point is the same. However, relying too heavily on personal relationships to win deals and grow the business does not scale well and can lead to a false sense of sound sales and marketing strategies or incorrect assessment of capabilities. An overreliance on relationships may actually mask mediocrity and underperformance in other areas. How often have you felt that despite suspected deficiencies of all sorts, you were still enjoying healthy growth and success? Your intuition is telling you that there are areas of your business that could be improved, but you may not be sure quite where to look.

Perhaps your company is losing ground against competitors and the pipeline is not looking as healthy. A common suspect is your pricing strategy. Assuming that you frequently lose on price might mask many other reasons for declining performance and may cause you to eat deeply into your profit margins when there may be other factors that are more relevant and easier to solve. It has been widely proven that just dropping your price rarely improves win rates over the long term. It is because you have now recalibrated your price, and the perceived value with it, to lower standards. It is against this backdrop of soundly predicting and planning for successful (i.e., profitable, repeatable, and stable) performance that we look closely at the factors involved in sales outcomes.

> *An overreliance on relationships may actually mask mediocrity and underperformance in other areas.*

There are multiple approaches available to assess how and why opportunities are won and lost within a company. Those approaches typically include primary market research, competitive intelligence gathering and analysis, and third-party-facilitated direct customer post-opportunity interviews. There are likely several formal and informal feedback channels that the product groups comb for additional insights. The often-overlooked (sometimes intentionally) component of this research is the insight to be gained directly from the front-line sellers.

The focus of this book is on gaining actionable competitive insights through the scalable process of quickly and effectively capturing win and loss information directly from those on the front lines who have the clearest view to the action—the sales force. This method of "crowd wisdom" is the power behind the insights captured from *seller-generated win/loss reviews*.[1] The method advocated here does not rely on a heavy-handed top-down approach, nor on one that has a single person or team responsible for harnessing and processing information into actionable insights. In fact, we're demonstrating how a grassroots, bottom-up approach of gathering and aggregating micro-intelligence provides some of the most accurate, relevant, and actionable insights that can benefit a broad group of stakeholders. The organization serves in an enabling and governing role to coordinate and democratize this process to maximize stakeholder value.

The benefits of gaining real-time information at the end of a sales cycle does not replace, but rather complements, those offered by broader marketing research studies, competitive intelligence reports, and customer surveys.

Here, the emphasis is on gaining immediate insights from the source most intimately familiar with your own company, your direct customer, and perhaps your customer's purchasing criteria—the seller. Understanding broader target customer perceptions about your company's products—how your broader customer base feels—falls primarily within the domain and expertise of the product and marketing groups. However, as we will discover, the information harnessed by the sales team should become an indispensible resource for augmenting and validating market surveys and competitive intelligence reports.

TRUSTING TODAY'S SELLER

Many sales performance and product management consultancies, including those that specialize in competitive intelligence, often dismiss the validity of seller-originated win/loss reviews. At some point in the past, this position may have been understandable and perhaps forgiven. Today, the sales profession is producing more sales consultants who are disciplined in understanding customer needs, more competent in guiding the customer's buying process, skilled at marshaling the resources necessary to strategically grow the customer's lifetime value, and taking more accountability for the outcomes of their sales efforts.

It is an unfortunate and pervasive perception that salespeople are not to be trusted with providing performance information that is believed to be largely accurate and actionable. The stereotype of the unscrupulous salesperson permeates pop culture and is continuously reinforced in iconic literary and cinematic works such as *Glengarry Glen Ross*.[2] An unfortunate consequence of this perpetuated stereotype is that there are many who have failed to recognize the elevated stature of the sales profession (and sales professionals) over the past 20 years, which is evolving toward more consultative selling. Increasing solution complexity, lengthening sales cycles, and smarter customers have necessitated a seller who is not only an expert in the sales profession, but an expert in his or her own products and industry.

Why, then, are sellers entrusted to represent and protect the interests of the company at its most visible interactions and vulnerable moments with its customers? When facing customers, salespeople are trained to shine the light on the strengths of their products and services while exposing the weaknesses of their competitors. This "skill" might find its way into how they assess their own performance. Internally, sellers will often shine the light on the strengths of their own performance while blaming weaknesses in pricing or products when they underperform. There is some validity to this argument. However, we should not confuse predisposition to biases with capability to assess business performance. It is in fact the seller who is uniquely positioned to capture the nuances of the factors related to the outcome. If a seller works within a culture of continuous learning and knows that the information he captures and shares will help put more money in his pockets while growing a larger share of the pie for his company, he is apt to call it like it is, and will align with the spirit of the process, if not the letter.

It is important to note, however, that qualitative data collection is prone to seller bias. Sellers will often attribute wins at some level to their team's business prowess and to all the people who supported them on the road to victory. However, losses are often attributed to factors such as pricing, product deficiencies, partner weaknesses, and the like. It is estimated that for wins, 75% of the time sellers will cite their selling or account management skills as among the primary reasons. By comparison, they will cite themselves as a contributing factor in the loss only 25% of the time.[3]

> *When asked whom they trusted for competitive insights, sellers ranked their peers well above other sources such as partners, product managers, and even their own competitive intelligence departments.*

Even so, this does not mean that important outcome insights are absent. We merely need to learn how to manage these biases. In later chapters, we will discuss why we must recognize, and even accommodate, these biases as they offer opportunities to uncover additional learning and insight. We'll also explore ways to discreetly neutralize seller bias while accurately revealing why deals are actually won or lost over time.

An interesting question to ask of sellers is whom *they* trust for information that helps them win deals. In an informal survey of over 200 salespersons, when asked whom they trusted for competitive insights, sellers ranked their peers well above other sources such as partners, product managers, and even their own competitive intelligence departments. The proliferation of information-sharing technologies and social networks also promotes a certain level of transparency and honesty. The expectation of peer review suggests the bias-neutralizing effect of providing information that is as accurate as possible, knowing that the primary consumers are those in their own role.

LISTEN TO THE CUSTOMER, TOO

Of course, many would argue that it is what the customer says that matters most, and ultimately it is! However, customers also have their biases and are not always forthcoming as to why you won or lost. Still, a seller may prefer to directly engage the customer if she sees an opportunity to mend strained relationships or build on executive-level relationships. Many customers and prospects who are in a position to provide feedback, especially in loss situations, simply avoid the exercise for fear of confrontation or having to explain their decision. Others may be under self-imposed nondisclosure as part of the request for proposal (RFP) conditions and process in an effort to continue receiving high-quality bids from the most reputable suppliers. The point is that there are many factors that can lead to biased customer feedback.

Conducting in-depth and direct postdeal customer debriefs is often facilitated by third-party consultants who specialize in this field. It is believed that a neutral party will entice the customer to reveal more than would be expected if directly approached by the sales team. These customer interviews usually go into great depth and detail and produce very insightful reports and analysis. Although consultants are positioned as neutral third parties, this does not guarantee unbiased feedback. The trained consultant can often detect bias and further probe in certain areas to cross-check other feedback for consistency.

DRIVING SCALE AND ACCURACY

The methods for conducting win/loss reviews advocated here apply to the spectrum of sales cycles of varying complexity and length—opportunities with short sales cycle time and simple buying decisions, or opportunities with longer cycles and more complex decision criteria. If we are to factor in simplicity, cost, timeliness, scalability and broad utility, getting post-opportunity feedback directly from the customer is not always a viable solution for gaining the insights within these constraints.

At some point the costs of collecting, analyzing, and reporting this information become greater than the value delivered.

If your company manages a thousand opportunities over the course of a fiscal year, how many of these would you consider worth the effort to hire a third party to go and interview: ten (1%), or a hundred of them (10%)? As the numbers of interviews go up, so do the costs. At some point the costs of collecting, analyzing, and reporting this information become greater than the value delivered. And while the information and insights are likely to have great depth, the insights from a limited sample may not be consumable and available across a broad set of stakeholders.

While offering greater depth and breadth of information, rarely will customer interviews offer the scale to derive statistically relevant results that can inform sales strategy and timely course correction. There may also be a lengthy gap between the time when the deal is won or lost and when the interview takes place and the information is analyzed and reported.

The audiences for the final reports generated by the customer interviews are often the senior leaders of companies who have the advanced skills and business acumen to understand them, and who are adept in interpreting complex analytics reports. The orientation and final recommendations from the reports may focus on only one group, for example, marketing managers or product managers. In some cases, the analysis is at such a depth that it may be difficult to interpret the insights in such a way that makes them actionable. Your author has experienced the spectrum of win/loss reviews and can attest to the variability in depth, quality, and intended audience.[4]

A NEW APPROACH

The information garnered from the seller-generated win/loss review process should complement, not replace, market and competitive intelligence reports, sales analytics, and direct customer interviews. However, it is important to differentiate between customer-engaged opportunity outcome reviews and those originated by the sales teams. For many who do not understand the approach, there is likely to be immediate suspicion raised at many levels. This reaction is natural as most customer feedback paradigms employed today (e.g., interviews, satisfaction surveys, focus groups, etc.) are still rooted in how business was historically done. The disruptive and transformative nature of information technology requires a new approach with the capabilities to reflect how business is being done *today*.

The disruptive and transformative nature of information technology requires a new approach with the capabilities to reflect how business is being done today.

The approach to win/loss reviews advocated here runs counter to conventional wisdom in the following fundamental ways:

Seller Generated versus Customer Debrief

Win/loss reviews depend primarily on the opportunity owner (individual or team) capturing and reporting relevant information on opportunity outcomes. As visualized in Figure 1.1, individual

FIGURE 1.1 Scale versus depth: Sellers generate high volumes of micro-intelligence. Customer interviews provide more depth but with lower volumes of micro-intelligence.

sellers or sales teams capture win/loss review information immediately after their own opportunity outcome is known. This contrasts with the lengthy but more detailed customer telephone interview that may be facilitated by a third party. For some, this will be difficult to accept, but our experience has repeatedly demonstrated that sellers actually do give the most accurate assessment of the forces affecting deal outcomes. Throughout the sales cycle, the seller is exposed to the buyer more than anyone else, and this information is often captured through the sales stages in the customer relationship management (CRM) system. As sellers' livelihoods depend on the customers they manage, it is in their interest to know everything about their customers and any environmental variables that can affect their performance with those customers.

A strategic or global account manager may have only one account to manage, and perhaps 90% of their time is spent actively managing that account and related activities. It is likely that they will have a great deal of knowledge about their customer; their decision-making criteria, competitors, and the orientation of key decision makers. Even if only 10% of their time is directed toward a particular customer, that is likely ten times more time than anyone else not directly associated with that account. As the seller orientation toward conducting win/loss reviews grows, what is expected from them will continue to improve, as will their outcome performance assessment.

Sales versus Marketing Orientation

The primary stakeholders being served by the win/loss reviews are the sales teams. Most often the point through which a customer engages with a company is through the front-line sellers. At this intersection, it makes sense that the seller is trained not only to deliver the value messages created by the product and marketing teams, but also to serve as the primary and ongoing conduit for customer feedback.

Through the several interactions that a seller has with his customer, facts, perceptions, and opinions are continually being exchanged between buyer and seller. Not only does this afford a more complete inventory of how the customer is reacting as you guide her through the buying cycle, but it also allows the seller to assess changes over time and to understand the sales dynamic. The seller is usually the one who best knows the *customer's customer* and can more accurately assess whether the solutions he is selling will help the customer meet *her* customer's demands. Understanding the customers that your customer serves adds a level of insight to what your customer's strategies are.

Many consultants in the field of product marketing and competitive intelligence will focus on the marketing department as the primary customer for the insights gathered from win/loss reviews. This has its merits as there is often a stronger orientation toward product performance and differentiation. It may also depend greatly on whether sales, marketing, or engineering owns product development in their portfolio. Product development is more often finding its way under the office of the chief executive

> *The seller is usually the one who best knows the customer's customer.*

officer. By placing the seller at the center of the "internal customer" list, the process design stays more aligned to the objective of increasing win rates, at higher value per opportunity, and at higher margins (lower cost of sale). This does not mean, however, that marketing and product development teams and other stakeholders will not benefit. On the contrary, they have more to gain as they will now have stronger line-of-sight feedback from their customer base.

Process Enabled versus Consultant Dependent

Advances in process science and technological innovations are placing more relevant information into the hands of those who need it, when they need it. Traditionally, a marketer needing performance trend information around a given set of products when certain environmental conditions exists might wait for months for information that is aggregated, formatted, and delivered; only then would the marketer be able to analyze and draw conclusions. That same person today need not wait for months, or even days, as information is immediately available and consumable. Advances in analytic and data visualization techniques found in widely available and specialized software packages are now within reach of the everyday knowledge worker.

To draw a simple analogy, many reading this book will remember when camera film needed to be developed by taking it to a local drugstore or a photo processing lab, or by mailing order. Sometime later, the prints were received along with the negatives nicely packaged in an envelope. Perhaps two prints were ordered, or larger-sized prints with glossy or matte finishes. Technology and process today have made this paradigm nearly obsolete for the average consumer. Digital cameras and smart devices such as Apple's iPod and Microsoft's Windows Phone 7 have consumerized technologies to the point where one can take as many pictures as desired, discard the unwanted ones, color correct, and send through email or directly post to a favorite social networking site. The traditional intermediary value is now built in. Today, many of those same intermediaries have shifted their focus to provide products and services that may still be out of reach for most do-it-yourself consumers. Consumers greatly benefit by hiring the expertise of others who provide posters, photo books, personalized coffee mugs, and a whole array of unique and personalized gifts.

In business, technology enables the surfacing and collection of actionable insights through robust and relevant reporting and business intelligence (BI) processes. The right business logic can effectively link the information with those stakeholders who seek it whenever necessary. Consulting experts provide the advanced expertise by helping interpret the win/loss review data and triangulate the insights with other feedback mechanisms such as direct customer surveys and competitive intelligence reports.

Continuous Insights versus Periodic Reports

At the speed with which market forces change, it is critical that actionable insights be captured and shared as close to real-time as possible. Relying only on periodic summaries that surface your strengths and weaknesses may lead to strategies or tactics that are outdated or fail to address emerging threats or opportunities. The state of technology today allows automated capabilities such as performance trending and forecasting, early alerts against performance specifications, and other key performance indicators that are capable of being monitored on an ongoing basis. Figure 1.2 conceptualizes and compares the relative time between insights and results.

When relying only on scorecards, one is looking at only a part of the picture, and typically at lagging indicators. By design, *scorecards* are primarily used for performance *management*, comparing results against targets, perhaps on a quarterly or annual basis. *Dashboards*, however, are a performance *monitoring* tool designed

Periodic Reports

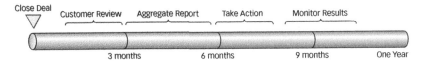

Real-Time Insights

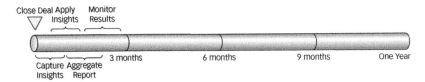

FIGURE 1.2   Time between Insights and Action

to look at a series of metrics that are in motion and moving relative to one another.

Using a metaphor that most adults are familiar with, every automobile has a dashboard, typically containing a speedometer, tachometer, fuel gauge, temperature gauge, oil pressure gauge, and charging system gauge. Each of these has some warning indicator, perhaps a sound or a light that signals that the systems they are monitoring are operating outside of safe operational limits. Failure to inspect a warning light, for example, might leave the motorist stranded on a highway. Typically, however, the responsible motorist takes immediate action to correct the condition causing the warning. Today, of course, automobiles can self-diagnose and even report warnings to their mechanic before the motorist knows that there is a problem. There may not even be a problem but a service light may remind the motorist to service the vehicle with proactive maintenance at regularly scheduled intervals.

Applying this concept to win/loss reviews is straightforward. The information received from customers through sales continuously feeds into the framework for capturing, analyzing, and reporting insights. Trends and other key performance indicators (KPIs) are continuously monitored for warning signals that permit corrective action on a timely basis.

Statistical Relevance versus Anecdotal Evidence

The ability to capture large volumes of relevant data makes it possible to scientifically test hypotheses about the dynamics driving your business. Establishing causal relationships between, for example, the win rates of a specific partner and those of a specific competitor might help a company by adjusting the partner strategies in a particular region. Or perhaps the testing revealed that in the western region, price/value was selected as a primary factor for winning, and that there were significant and sustained successes over a competitor that is stronger in other regions. With price being equal across all regions, knowledge of how the western region was delivering its value proposition might be portable to other regions. At the same time, statistics can also be instrumental in rejecting hypotheses that were previously based only on anecdotal evidence.

The ability to scale to a much wider set of opportunities, defined by predetermined business rules, allows for statistically relevant measurements, finer granularity, data stratification, and more accurate conclusions. A system that can harness large volumes of data that allow for hypothesis tests for causal correlations between factors and outcomes, or the interplay between the factors themselves, will provide the confidence needed to reach sound conclusions. Anecdotal insights revealed from direct customer interviews are more relevant to that specific customer and for a specific situation. Typically, too few customer reviews are conducted to achieve a sample size from which to derive sound, data-driven conclusions.

SUMMARY

- Knowing why a company wins or loses business is critical for driving business performance beyond organic growth.
- Several factors contribute to opportunity outcomes, many within our control, and understanding the correlations of these factors leads to actions that reduce risks.
- Relying too heavily on personal relationships does not scale and leaves the company vulnerable to strategic risks.
- Pricing is a common suspect for losing, but adjusting prices downward also downward-adjusts perceived value. Pricing strategies alone do not necessarily equate to winning more business.
- There are multiple approaches for conducting win/loss reviews, but the most commonly overlooked method is that which originates from the front-line sellers.
- Sellers today have deeper expertise in the area they represent, are more accustomed to consultative sales techniques, and have the clearest view to the customer's decision criteria.
- Biases in evaluating post-deal outcomes are present in all win/loss methodologies. Seller biases should be accommodated, but can later be neutralized.
- Sellers will typically trust information that is generated by their front-line peers over any other intelligence source.
- Customer interviews have their benefits and can be a part of the win/loss review information gathering process. These are typically facilitated by third-party consultants specializing in this area.
- Having a scalable process for win/loss reviews ensures that information is truly representative of the population, and not merely of a select few outcomes.
- The five key differentiators of field-generated win/loss reviews are that they originate from the seller, are oriented primarily from the sales point of view, are process enabled, provide continuous data and monitoring, and yield high volumes of data that permit hypothesis testing by statistical analysis.

NOTES

1. J. Surowiecki, *The Wisdom of Crowds* (New York: Anchor Books, 2005). The phenomenon of crowdsourcing brilliantly described in Surowiecki's book can be applied to win/loss reviews, as it places the emphasis on the individual for the micro-insights while aggregating these insights into macro views.

2. D. A. Mamet, *Glengarry Glen Ross*. This 1982 play (later made into an iconic film) portrays the sales agents and their manager resorting to illegal and unethical sales practices.

3. Richard M. Schroder, *From a Good Sales Call to a Great Sales Call* (New York: McGraw Hill, 2011).

4. Perhaps it is a characteristic quality of this relatively nascent area of business intelligence that it creates confusion around what is actually meant by win/loss reviews. This is compounded by some variations in terminology. *Win/loss reviews* and *win/loss analysis* are often used interchangeably to describe the general process of conducting post-opportunity outcome collection and analysis. A quick Internet search on the topic shows many areas where this discipline applies. In addition to considering the application for post-opportunity outcomes, it can be found in understanding website purchase behaviors, sports events (e.g., baseball and horseracing), and gaming (e.g. casino table games).

CHAPTER 2

WIN/LOSS REVIEWS AND BUSINESS INTELLIGENCE

I not only use all the brains that I have, but all that I can borrow.

—Woodrow Wilson

The term *business intelligence* was first coined in 1958 by Hans Peter Luhn, an IBM researcher. In his paper, "A Business Intelligence System," Luhn defines *intelligence* as "the ability to apprehend the interrelationships of presented facts in such a way as to guide action towards a desired goal."[1] Applied to win/loss reviews, business intelligence (BI) looks at the factors (i.e., the facts) that drove known outcomes, and seeks to apply these intrinsically correlated factors toward the actions necessary to achieve the desired outcome (i.e., the goal).

Today, BI is an often-used term for the capability to draw information and insights derived from a vast collection of transactional and market data. Too often BI is considered the domain of business planners, decision makers, and huge information technology (IT) departments. However, BI no longer requires huge data warehouses or IT systems with extensive computational capabilities. Smaller, more powerful, and more agile IT platforms are replacing the heavy equipment that needs specialized operators and infrastructure. Technological advances have also made the analysis of data much easier and more powerful and accessible. The rise of "self-service BI" means that the benefits of BI can be enjoyed by a wider audience and in ways that are more user-driven and defined. This clear intention to turn away from dependence on consultants and IT–dependent BI process is part of what is also driving the evolution and flattening of many business architectures. A win/loss review system is one of a number of growing processes that are becoming more personalized and rapidly fulfilling the promise and vision of BI.

The rise of "self-service BI" means that the benefits of BI can be enjoyed by a wider audience.

One of the distinguishing characteristics of the win/loss review process as opposed to traditional BI processes is that much of the information harnessed is generated, reported, and consumed directly by the field sales force while equally benefiting a much broader set of stakeholders. The ability of those who are in closest contact with their customers to capture a rich mixture of structured and unstructured data is providing new ways for sales and marketing teams to observe, record, and interact with their business and competitive environment.

Whether capturing information as part of an integrated customer relationship management (CRM) process, or an offline application, or even a mobile phone app, the opportunities for capturing information when it is happening are all around. At the same time, the opportunity for finding relevant and timely information is better than ever before. Think about the last time you looked at a periodical that was more than six months old and thought that it was out of date, or saw an online article or blog that was only a month old and thought that it was too late to comment on it. BI capabilities are now reaching the level that allows us to connect with the right information at the right time, around our needs.

The nature of this *just-in-time* research paradigm that is becoming more mainstream at the user level suggests that the process takes on characteristics more descriptive of business analytics (BA), which is oriented toward ad-hoc analysis of past deal outcomes and is focused on interactive and investigative analysis by end users to derive new insights.[2] What is searched for and analyzed will depend greatly on the characteristics of the active opportunities being managed. The attributes can be a function of the influencing categories (e.g., competitors, relationships, products, services, and partners) and can be further broken down into more granular factors within each category. The capabilities of our computer systems are making this level of granularity possible.

The discipline of forensic sales is examining the evidence of the factors that led to a sales outcome, and creating a new knowledge base from which to derive and apply the insights gained.[3] Further application of insights gained by reviewing the evidence depends on the stakeholder requirements. The front-line seller will have different needs than, say, the product manager. Still, it is important to note here that we are still using the same source data that was originally captured by the sales teams. This "capture once, use often" paradigm will need to be pervasive if we are to normalize the baseline data and taxonomy, and draw consistent and complementary conclusions that serve a broad set of stakeholders.

The capabilities of self-service BI allow a wider range of users to define their information views and obtain early insights to their business without having to get technical help from the IT department. Indeed this is the direction of BI.

Leading industry analysts are pointing to growing demand across businesses for making data more discoverable and enhanced with new visualization techniques that tell a story with richer graphics, instead of just words and numbers. And when a user finds a view she likes, having the ability to save this personalized view and share it with others opens new horizons for collaborating on business performance and competitive intelligence. This same capability benefits a wide range of users with different requirements.

A NEW KNOWLEDGE MODEL

By placing personalized BI capabilities out of IT and in the hands of the ordinary user, analysis and decision making are more in harmony across the organization as there is "one version of the truth," as everyone is working from shared data sources. Of course, the actual views one may create may vary widely, but as long as we are querying the same source data, the quality and consistency of the decisions and conclusions are likely to be more aligned within and across stakeholder groups. Figure 2.1 illustrates this concept as applied to win/loss reviews and emphasizes the information flow from field sales, further reuse by multiple stakeholders, and the return to field sales. It is important to point out that the CRM systems today are capable of fully integrating the win/loss review process, although the figure separates it for model clarity.

By combining sales performance data with data captured from the win/loss reviews, the reasons behind those trends, and potential remedies for emerging risks, sales teams have greater insights in to what is going in their business. Sales teams can also create custom views of the win–rate trends against specific competitors in their region, no longer relying on only broader competitive trends. The granularity continues beyond competitors, but can also be viewed by products, partners, and even individuals. At the same time, sales teams are able to instantly take advantage of knowledge created by other teams across the world. One of the most common requests by sales teams is the ability to share tactical knowledge related to

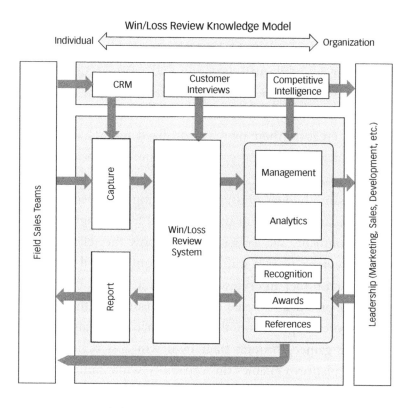

FIGURE 2.1 Knowledge Model of a Win/Loss Review Process

specific sales scenarios that can be leveraged. These are not necessarily the ubiquitous "best practices" that are often positioned for broad consumption and applicability, but rather the *effective* practices that address a specific need at a point in time. The aggregation of the same source information feeds the product marketing and development teams, with perhaps a stronger focus on campaign and product performance.

As businesses of all sizes and from all industries apply increasingly advanced business modeling techniques to compete in an increasingly competitive environment, the data required also grows

Sales teams are able to instantly take advantage of knowledge created by other teams across the world.

in complexity. Paradoxically, we're now expected to be able to analyze much higher volumes of data, turn that into actionable information, all while making faster and more accurate business decisions. Adding to the challenge is the freezing or even reduction of IT and analyst staff that would often assist the business owners in creating their own personalized reports and analytics tools. Standard, static, one-size-fits-all reports are no longer adequate to manage a business.

These same budget pressures are driving the need for greater innovation and reliance on the individual for managing his business environment. We earlier discussed how the seller-generated win/loss reviews mark a shift from the conventional third-party-facilitated customer interviews. This trend is partially driven by the budget pressures to scale back on outsourcing these services, placing more emphasis on the sellers to capture and share the knowledge gained through their own win/loss reviews. A self-service BI platform enables this capability while hiding the complexities of the IT infrastructure.

The arrival of a new competitor may not be known until an opportunity is lost in a competitive battle.

A well-designed process will provide compelling visualizations and filtering techniques, and the front-end capture process can be an equally compelling and enabling experience. Using browser-based interfaces with simple pick lists, checkboxes, radio buttons, and freeform text areas simplifies the process of capturing information while offering a structured process that normalizes data creation from the outset, nearly eliminating data hygiene issues down the road. Where applicable, additional "tool-tips" and help guides can be embedded for context-sensitive user support.

As new market entrants to the competitive field increase, so does the need to have an agile system that can quickly recognize and begin capturing information about them. Prior to the capabilities we have today, adding a new competitor to the standard list might take several months before the competitor was recognized in any reporting system. If the competitor did not conform to an existing business classification or taxonomy, it could even take years. The arrival of a new competitor may not be known until an opportunity is lost in a competitive battle. Today, a new competitor in a market can be quickly added to the win/loss review system, which then allows immediate recognition that there is a new player in town. As this competitor is now in the system, performance against that competitor can be monitored and experiences captured and shared. Consider how often a company was caught unaware of a competitor that was taking significant market share until it was pointed out by analysts two years later. Had the front-line sellers been empowered to raise the early alert, these situations could have been detected much sooner.

BI GOVERNANCE

Pushing this much power to the end user will often put executives on edge, as there are inherent risks. It is therefore important that any system allowing this level of user interaction has its safeguards against security breaches, data vandalism, and leaks of company confidential information. Governance and monitoring of user activities are necessary, especially since we are now allowing access to information by persons or groups who may not be formally trained in how to manage this newly discovered power. Typically, however, the design would never allow end users to get that close to the source data unless they are the ones creating it. For querying, reporting, and analyzing purposes, the broader users are often placed in a sort of "sandbox" where they are free to explore and play, isolated from the data warehouses containing the source data. What they are using is essentially a copy of the data; or their queries are modulated in such a way that they prevent errant or poorly designed queries from overloading the data servers and affecting system-wide performance.

Another governance practice is to enforce user-based security access controls to different parts of the data. A seller, for example, will need to access the capture and reporting components of a win/loss review tool, but may not need access to the analytics or management components. A sales manager, however, can be given access to the management components where more sensitive company confidential information resides. A product manager may be given access to the reports to query information on specific products and their features, while a competitive intelligence manager might have access to the reports and analytics, but not the capture or management components. The access rights depend on the needs of the business and the design of the process as well as the tolerance for risk.

For a win/loss review system, governance policies may be too strict and be counterproductive to process and may significantly reduce the benefits. For example, one of the critical success factors of a seller-oriented win/loss review program is that sellers be able to learn from their peers in other parts of the country or across the world. Tying down the system to the point where a seller can view information only about his own territory, or worse, his own accounts, would negate the benefits realized at the front line. Even the upstream stakeholders would suffer as the quality of information capture would suffer since the seller would have no visibility into how the information is being used elsewhere.

PROVIDERS OF SELF-SERVICE BI

Companies today have many choices for implementing self-service BI solutions that support a robust win/loss review program. Most of the major players in the space offer enhancements to their flagship products to make BI more accessible to the broader user base.

Tibco Software, QlikTech, and Tableau are relatively new companies offering simplified BI tools. Major BI vendors like Microsoft, IBM Cognos, SAP, and Oracle offer a wide range of solutions for varying company sizes and budgets. There are also several open-source offerings that usually require specialized integration and support services and may lack the integrated security features required by major corporations.

A company may also consider putting its win/loss review process in the cloud. Advances in software as a service (SaaS), platform as a service (PaaS), and infrastructure as a service (IaaS) capabilities provide the benefits of a managed and secure environment while offering users—at any time and from anywhere—access to information. All of the previously referenced BI companies have cloud versions of their BI solutions, whose benefits will greatly extend the utility of a win/loss review program.

POCKET BI: INTELLIGENCE TO GO

The advances in mobile technology and user interfaces are also making BI widely available as a mobile app. The popular and widespread usage of smartphones for personal and professional use, from Apple, Microsoft, Google, RIM, and others, are truly making BI portable.

Microsoft has embraced this capability by developing the Win/ Loss Review Mobile App (see Figure 2.2) for its employees worldwide. For example, an employee on her way to a customer meeting can gain additional insights into how her peers won opportunities against a particular competitor. Of course, the information on the smartphone is coming from the exact same data source as that on her laptop or desktop computer. Only the form factor has changed.

The ability for smartphone manufacturers to deliver secure enterprise applications over mobile carriers is offering many usage scenarios barely imagined just a few years ago.

FIGURE 2.2   Win/Loss Review Mobile App

FROM BI TO COMPETITIVE INTELLIGENCE

In the growing field of competitive intelligence (CI), the insights derived from a win/loss review program enabled by a robust BI platform should contribute to any CI portfolio of sources, tools, and analytical methods. In some cases, information garnered from a win/loss review program may form the bulk of the competitive information, whereas in other cases it may be but one of many sources to draw upon.

While this book leaves an in-depth discussion of the CI profession to its expert practitioners, it emphasizes the emerging importance of the role that a formal CI program plays while drawing a parallel to the challenges that a formal win/loss review program faces of becoming broadly institutionalized.

The appetite for static, sequential, and disconnected information is wearing thin.

In his book *Proven Strategies in Competitive Intelligence*, John E. Prescott notes that "too many businesses still have not incorporated CI into their organizational structure and corporate culture, much less into their IT framework (i.e., establishing an interactive CI area within their corporate intranet and making it accessible throughout the organization, from the CEO to the sales reps)."[4] Important to emphasize here is the concept of accessibility of the information so that an organization can utilize it in an effective and coordinated manner. The theme of transparency and accessibility is pervasive throughout this text.

With the proliferation of social media networks and Web-based and mobile-carrier streaming media, consumers and businesses are changing how information and entertainment is being consumed. It is no secret that the traditional media formats of television, print, and radio are seeing their audiences shift to media that promote interactivity, community, and contribution (not only consumption). This phenomenon is having profound effects on how companies are communicating with their employees (see also Chapter 8, "Stakeholder and Cultural Considerations").

Employees are increasingly relying on internal and external peer networks for information relevant to their role. Similar to the phenomenon sweeping the media outlets, employees are demanding more insights from their peers, want real-time information, and look for opportunities to contribute to the collective body of knowledge. These expectations are placing tremendous pressure on traditional internal information sources and formats such as competitive playbooks and product positioning guides. Merely changing the form factor of these artifacts by converting them to digital format (e.g., Word, PowerPoint, Acrobat, etc.) or putting them on an internal Web page doesn't go far enough.

Our competitive business world is playing out in real time, and the appetite for static, sequential, and disconnected information is wearing thin. By their nature, sellers in a competitive situation are emotionally driven and engaged. To illustrate this point, consider team sporting events of all kinds where teams gather before a game to intensify their winning spirit through some ritual. It is likely, too, that teams expend considerable effort learning about their opponents' strengths and weaknesses while finding ways to exploit vulnerabilities based on their own capabilities. Much of the learning and building of knowledge comes from individuals who have a piece of competitive knowledge and insights that they share with their teammates. When combined, these valuable bits of knowledge begin to inform competitive strategy.

SUMMARY

- BI is no longer a business tool for planners and decision makers, but is now a mainstream asset for nearly everyone who needs it.
- Win/loss review data contributes to BI and is further enriched by the field sales teams who capture the data and insights.
- Process and technology are allowing just-in-time research paradigms and information to be used in multiple ways, eliminating redundant and inefficient data capture methods. This reflects the "capture once, use often" paradigm.
- Forensic sales means examining the evidence of the factors that led to a sales outcome in order to create a new knowledge base from which to derive and apply the insights gained.
- The capabilities of self-service BI now allow a wider range of users to define their information views and obtain early insights to their business.
- "One version of the truth" means that everyone is working from the same data sources.
- Teams are expected to be able to analyze much higher volumes of data while making faster and more accurate business decisions.
- Agile systems allow end users to contribute to the data taxonomy, permitting earlier identification and tracking of new market entrants.
- Governance models are evolving to keep pace with the capabilities of the democratization of information.

- A rich set of BI providers are offering new ways to access, view, and share BI. Many are taking advantage of Web-based and mobile-carrier technologies to make BI more portable.
- Institutionalizing competitive intelligence initiatives can leverage BI to gain wider support.

NOTES

1. H. P. Luhn, "A Business Intelligence System," *IBM Journal of Research and Development*, 2(4), 1958, 314–319.
2. M. Beller and A. Barnett, "Next Generation Business Analytics Technology Trends," [presentation] Lightship Partners, LLC, 2009. Creative Commons Attribution–Share Alike 3.0 Unported License.
3. The term *forensic sales* is introduced here to raise awareness of this emerging discipline and to elevate its place among the scientific disciplines and professions adopting forensics for gathering and analyzing evidence related to sales performance.
4. John E. Prescott, *Proven Strategies in Competitive Intelligence* (New York: John Wiley & Sons, 2001).

CHAPTER 3

WHY DO WE WIN OR LOSE?

For every action there is an equal and opposite competitor.
—Business proverb

Over the course of a fiscal month, quarter, or year, your company may have hundreds or thousands of opportunities that flow through the sales pipeline. A lot of work goes into what ultimately turns into a sale, or a lost piece of business. Most businesses that actually track the outcomes of their opportunities categorize opportunities in two outcome categories: wins and losses. From here, it is a fairly simple calculation to understand the win rate with this base level of information. However, win rates tell only part of the story and can be further refined by looking at win-rate performance by geography or product line, for example.

Often, losses simply signal the exit of the opportunity from the pipeline without considering whether there is an opportunity to plan to win back the deal (the *winback* plan) or, at minimum, to capture key learnings from the experience. Perhaps losses are never fully declared as such, and are just left in limbo status in your

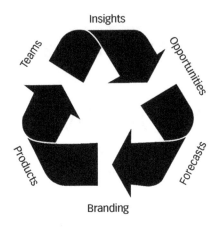

Insights

Teams

Opportunities

Products

Forecasts

Branding

FIGURE 3.1   Recycling Insights from a Renewable Intelligence Source

customer relationship management (CRM) system. Borrowing an ecological metaphor and graphic (see Figure 3.1), there exists a great opportunity to recycle this information waste into a renewable intelligence source!

Research suggests that fewer than 5% of companies apply any formal sort of win/loss review discipline to their sales outcomes. Those that do them often focus only on the losses. Wins are often broadly recognized through internal emails, but lack the formal structure that enables the benefits of a properly conducted and shared review to be realized.

FACTORS CONTRIBUTING TO WINS AND LOSSES

Depending on whom you ask, there are many reasons or factors that contribute to an opportunity outcome. These factors can be grouped into categories to help direct the input from the sales teams. Figure 3.2 provides an example of win/loss factors broadly categorized into intuitive groupings that permit the seller to quickly classify the opportunity outcome while allowing management and other stakeholders to draw insights from a normalized

Offering	Relationship	Competitiveness	Services	Other
❏ Alignment with Needs ❏ Price/Value Proposition ❏ Product Features ❏ Strength of Solution	❏ Account Management ❏ BDM/TDM Changes ❏ Political Alignment ❏ Relationship Health	❏ Customer References ❏ Customer Evidence ❏ Differentiated Solution ❏ Incumbent Supplier/ Internal Skills	❏ Partner Expertise and Capability ❏ Partner Presence/ Availability ❏ Strength of Service and Support	❏ Merger/ Acquisition ❏ Regulatory Issues

FIGURE 3.2   Sample Categories and Factors

data set. In addition, an institutionalized win/loss review program will quickly reveal where there are strengths and weaknesses in the company's offerings, sales capabilities, competitive position, partnering strategies, and other areas affecting performance.

It is important to note that identifying the categories and factors for any business should be a collaborative effort among the corporate teams, the sales teams, and the marketing/product teams. Factors can differ based on a variety of opportunity criteria but they should be restricted to five or less within any given category for ease of identification and selection. There can also be several specialized categories depending on the specialized industries or customer segments that are served. For example, doing business with governments may involve several other factors (e.g., political considerations, funding sources, channel regulations, procurement policies, etc.) that are not normally considered with private sector businesses.

Evidence of these factors can be explicitly stated or documented (e.g., "Your proposal was selected on its cost relative to the value being provided") or anecdotal through customer conversations or information known to your channel partner. In most cases, however, the account manager will have personal knowledge through the multiple interactions he has had with the customer or partner as he managed the opportunity through the sales stages. One could argue that this of course depends on having a sales organization that is capable of influencing, or at least knowing, how decisions are made and what the buying criteria are. Knowing what these factors are should not be something to discover after the deal is won or lost.[1]

With some exceptions, the win and loss factors should be bimodal. For example, your company can win a deal due primarily to a price/value proposition, whereas the same factor causes your competitor to lose a deal. In a typical win scenario, the customer may have perceived your price/value proposition as the primary factor over your competitor. This, of course, assumes that price/value was the primary factor. We say "primary factor" to acknowledge that there are likely several factors affecting the outcome of an opportunity. In most cases, however, there are usually one or two factors that have the most impact on the outcome. Other primary factors such as relationship health or competitive differentiation should also work both ways—they can be the reason for the win *or* the loss. As stated earlier, however, it is likely that there are several contributing factors.

When constructing your specific framework for the factors, use this simple rule of thumb: The same factor should be applicable for the win or the loss. If the factors for losses cannot also be applied for wins, they are likely an *excuse* for losses. An easy way to check this is to use an actual deal from your business that was recently lost, and ask whether your reason for this loss might actually be the same reason why your competitor won. If it isn't, it is likely an excuse. There are exceptions to this rule, of course.

It's important to allow for this bimodal approach because as you apply other deal components, patterns might surface that wouldn't otherwise be noticeable. For instance, if a price/value proposition is the primary win reason for a solution sale into the banking industry, but it is also the primary loss reason for the same solution sale into the insurance industry, we can use the insights gained within the banking industry to potentially influence the future performance within the insurance industry.

> *If the factors for losses cannot also be applied for wins, they are likely* an excuse *for losses.*

For purposes of uncovering statistically relevant correlations, it is important that the factors be normalized and clearly defined. In addition, business rules may require that only the top two or three factors be selected so as to not dilute the factor correlations against the outcomes with too many selections.

One could argue that there are actually hundreds of factors that contribute to a specific outcome, and there are. However, the law of diminishing returns quickly takes hold as the marginal output, in this case the insights returned, significantly decreases as we add more units of input. Research strongly suggests that the selection of three factors is the maximum for any given deal. And even though several factors may have had some influence on the deal outcome, not all of them need be invoked as being influential on the outcome.

IS A WIN ALWAYS A WIN?

Perhaps owing to the drive to achieve a win as the ultimate goal, there may be a tendency to overlook what sacrifices had to be made to get the win. "Win at all costs" is a dangerous mantra and, unfortunately, in the drive for market share or penetration, we see it play out time and again. It is common business practice to construct special or exceptional offers to do what is necessary to win a piece of the business in order to secure a foothold with a new client, or expand into new offerings for existing clients. A good example is the drastically discounted product or service, often referred to as a *loss leader*, offered well below what it would normally cost to be profitable. There are many other deal "sweeteners" or negotiated concessions that can push the cost of a sale to the point where it becomes unprofitable—an extended pilot period, a complex proof of concept, free upgrades, discounted maintenance and support, and so on. When used judiciously and sparingly, these tactics can be an effective way to secure future business. However, when exercised regularly and without proper governance, discipline, and empowerment guidelines, there exists potential for abuse that could quickly drive a company out of business. At some point, those costs will need to be recovered.

A detailed anatomy of a "win" and what determines the quality of that win is beyond the scope of this book as there are several domain-specific variables—profit margins, cost of sale, sales model, productivity metrics, and so on—that are best defined by the specific businesses. However, a properly implemented win/loss review program can provide the important markers that assist businesses in determining the quality of wins.

NARRATIVES PROVIDE ADDITIONAL CONTEXT

A more effective win/loss review process also allows for the collection of short narratives from the sales teams that support, clarify, and enhance the factors selected. By providing a way to capture the thoughts of the opportunity owner or sales team, these narratives build a short story, or narrative, that makes it easier to understand the dynamics of a particular outcome since additional context is now provided. Figure 3.3 demonstrates how the short narratives support the factors selected.

Referencing our earlier discussion of the number of factors to select, if too many factors are selected, it will likely follow that either the narrative is disconnected from them or the narrative

Factors Selected	Deal Summary	Key Challenges	How Challenges Were Addressed
√ Strength of solution √ Customer references	Energy exploration BI solution for senior management utilizing existing data platform	Customer wanted to leverage existing platform, and required strong prior industry adoption before committing	Able to leverage existing data through a Proof of Concept (using existing Web Services). Also provided 3 noncompetitive reference customers (Contoso, EEX Solutions, and BEX). The Customer contacted Contoso and BEX, confirming our stated capabilities.

FIGURE 3.3   Building the Narrative around the Outcome Factors

becomes too long and cumbersome. The narrative should be very short and concise.

FACTOR WEIGHTING

In some industries we may wish to know as much detail as possible, meaning that they encourage the selection of as many factors as possible, perhaps ten or more, for each deal outcome. One mechanism to accommodate this business requirement is a factor weighting system. For example, on a five-point scale where a 5 carries the most weight, price/value might score a 3, whereas being the incumbent supplier might have scored a 5, and so on. This allows for more complex algorithms to fine-tune the analysis and insights. When thinking of using this ranking system, keep in mind that it may not be optimal from a collection and reporting scenario as it requires additional time from the sales team to estimate the level of impact of each factor. This may not be feasible in a collection and reporting scenario for the sales teams who are looking for fast and effective clues to help them win their next deal. We'll look at this in more detail in Chapter 4, "Capturing the Data."

DO WE LEARN MORE FROM WINS OR LOSSES?

Some would argue that losses present a greater opportunity than wins to learn and to apply these lessons to future opportunities. However, it is often through the process of winning that the evidence for the outcome is more clearly understood. Wins are often more valuable as there is more ongoing customer engagement that may permit additional harnessing of insights. For example, and especially in complex deals, being awarded a deal may allow for deeper understanding of the customer's buying decision criteria as you get into the detailed scoping and final terms and conditions. This is knowledge territory that a losing competitor simply does not get to enjoy.

Different individuals and companies place different emphasis on wins and losses. However, it is only through a fair and equal assessment of both wins and losses that true trends can be developed and insight gained that can benefit future sales efforts. Losses present an interesting opportunity to identify areas of risk exposure within a company, specifically in branding and products, pricing or presentation strategies, partner relationships, sales team effectiveness, and so forth. Wins represent the opposite. They often highlight individuals, teams, or organizations that are most effective at assisting in deal closure and use approaches to customers that work. By bringing both of those together a company is better able to assess its opportunity performance, make course corrections, and exploit its strengths for long-lasting benefit.

Myth: Teams learn more from their losses than from wins.
Fact: Both wins and losses are fertile ground for learning and carry the same potential for revealing valuable insights.

DISENGAGED OPPORTUNITIES: WHAT'S THE REAL STORY?

There is yet another type of outcome that is broadly referred to as a "disengaged," "no-decision," or "walk-away" opportunity. These are deals that are removed from the pipeline forecast for reasons other than a win or loss. From a win/loss review perspective, disengaged opportunities should include only *qualified* opportunities that were part of the active pipeline but were removed or deactivated before they could run their natural course to either a win or a loss outcome. Here, we stress *qualified* to differentiate from the bulk of the opportunities that are generated by marketing campaigns, but that were not passed on to the sales organization for qualification. Our research shows that where disengaging (or some variant definition) is allowed, sales teams may actually disengage between 50% and 70% of their qualified opportunities, leaving behind a potentially sizable amount of revenue and new customers (and share) for their competitors to enjoy.

There are actually valid reasons why someone would disengage from an opportunity. In many cases, leads and unqualified opportunities originating from marketing activities may have prematurely found their way into a sales pipeline, creating noise and requiring wasteful cycles to weed them out at the expense of nurturing qualified opportunities. The situation could also exist where a qualified opportunity is being pursued but the customer provides notification that it has lost funding, is being taken over, or the like. In this case it is realistic to disengage.

Apart from having very valid reasons for disengaging from opportunities, a high percentage of disengaged opportunities can be symptomatic of other issues. The point in the sales cycle at which deals are disengaged can also be a strong indicator of pipeline management competence, team discipline, or cultural considerations (see Figure 3.4). Analysis of disengaged opportunities could yield some

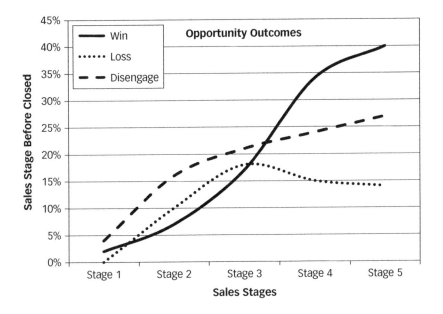

FIGURE 3.4   Sales Stage Immediately before Outcome

very interesting results. It could highlight issues with the qualification process being followed or the lead-generation process, or even expose a corporate sales culture where it is better to disguise a loss as disengaged rather than calling it what it is and learning from it.

If a high number of deals are disengaged in the latter stages in their cycle, it could mean that they are really lost deals masked as disengaged, or that faulty assumptions were made about the probability of winning, or that the deals were not really qualified to begin with. For many disengaged deals, it will be best to classify them as losses and to apply the rigor around reviewing them as a lost deal. Depending on the industry, deal size, competitor, and so forth, there can be an established set of criteria that guide what can be considered a disengaged deal.

Distinguished from wins and losses, disengaged opportunities will have their own set of outcome factors. The example disengaged factors in Figure 3.5 are separated into two main categories: customer initiated and company initiated.

Customer Initiated	Company Initiated
❏ Budget Frozen/Cut	❏ Capability to Deliver Solution
❏ Priorities Shifted	❏ Low Return on Investment
❏ Limited Invitations to Bid	❏ Potential to Win
❏ Supplier Disqualification	❏ Duplicate Opportunity
	❏ Other

FIGURE 3.5   Categories and Factors of Disengaged Opportunities

The primary differentiator between the two categories is the level of control one has in each decision and the potential next steps for that opportunity. *Customer-initiated disengagements* have less chance of resurrecting into a viable opportunity if there is strong supporting evidence. *Company-initiated disengaged factors* are more within the seller's control. Although these may also be valid reasons, sellers often disengage too soon from what could otherwise have been a win or a loss. It is the sales manager with strong skills and business acumen who can spot future business opportunities within the disengaged opportunities.

DELAYED DEALS BENEFIT FROM WIN/LOSS REVIEWS

Whereas the focus of this book is on learning from opportunity outcomes, the same framework is applicable and quite relevant to *active* deals that have slipped past their intended close date. As we saw at the beginning of Chapter 1, the discipline of win/loss reviews applies not only to improving business performance, but also to improving our capability to *predict* outcomes. In sales, this speaks directly to our ability to manage to an accurate forecast. For marketers, this might focus on predicting market share growth.

Anyone who has managed a sales pipeline knows that the actual deals that ultimately close in a given quarter do not always match what was forecast at the start of that quarter. Sales teams with stalled deals may actually close the deal well into the next quarter. This often manifests itself in consistently inaccurate and wide variances of actuals versus forecasts.

Often, however, the risks of stalled deals are mitigated by having a sort of buffer of deal upsides that are not forecasted in the current quarter, but that may have an opportunity to close in that quarter if accelerated. "Bluebirds," those deals in managed accounts that seemingly come from nowhere, often form part of the buffer that helps mitigate the risks to forecast accuracy. For example, in reviewing forecast accuracy, you may have a quarterly tolerance level of plus or minus 5%. This is a common sales target across many industries. When composed only of your known forecasted pipeline, your accuracy may have a 20% variance, plus or minus. You know from experience, however, that the potential upsides on existing deals, accelerated deals, plus bluebirds narrow the variance to nearly 3% every quarter. You might be able to manage your pipeline in this manner since you know the nuances of your business and are able to apply your vast stores of tacit knowledge to business and sales management.

Others may not have this capability, especially those new to management and/or new to the accounts they are managing. Consistently performing outside of these boundaries, especially on the low side, may trigger other sales and marketing processes that look at better deal qualification and forecasting. If actual figures are consistently "blowing the numbers out of the water," this, too, can indicate that there may be growth potential not being fully realized, but instead being left to chance. This often leads those in the sales organization to think managers are intentionally underforecasting, often referred to as "sandbagging," which is done to create the appearance of consistently overdelivering on commitments. This game is sometimes played by weaker sales managers who are not meeting their quota but look to enhance their image by exceeding their forecasts. Whether in the positive or negative zones, wide and sustained variances may sometimes have management looking at specific individuals for performance improvement plans.

So, what might be a leading indicator of a healthy and accurate forecast? Pipeline *coverage* and pipeline *velocity* are two of the most common. Pipeline coverage looks at the aggregated deal values and determines whether and by how much they fill the revenue gap. Pipeline velocity measures the relative speed, usually measured in number of days or months, with which deals move through each stage of the sales process. The tolerable limits are dependent on the industry and the complexity of the solutions being sold.

Applying the same principles for wins and losses, delayed deals might have factors all their own causing their delay in closing on a timely basis. While not technically lost deals, delayed deals run a higher risk of not closing. The delay may be self-inflicted if the sales team didn't deliver commitments to the prospect in time. Perhaps the deal is with an existing customer, but the deployment of the prior solution is way behind schedule and the customer thinks it best to wait. Often, the delay is an intentional tactic by the customer to win concessions in the final negotiations. Perhaps your competitors have started to make noise with irrational counteroffers, sensing that they had little chance of winning the deal, anyway. An opportunity languishing or suspended in any particular stage makes the customer an easy target for competitors to influence their decision criteria.

The point is that understanding the factors, as with wins and losses, is critical to move the deal forward toward a successful outcome. Collectively understanding the forces that lead to delays can provide key learning that can be taken straight back to the field so that deals can regain an acceptable velocity.

> *An opportunity languishing or suspended in any particular stage makes the customer an easy target for competitors to influence their decision criteria.*

SUMMARY

- Reviewing the hundreds or thousands of opportunities that flow through your pipeline in each time period offers valuable insights into your business performance.
- Fewer than 5% of companies apply any formal win/loss review discipline to their sales outcomes, and those that do usually focus only on the losses.
- Information recycling can create a new source for competitive intelligence.
- Multiple factors contribute to opportunity outcomes and can be normalized and categorized for selection and reporting.
- Factors should be bimodal, and they should be the same for a win as for a loss.
- Short narratives around the opportunity, its challenges, and the solutions to the challenges provide context to the opportunity factors and data.
- Factor weighting can be used to assign relative influences toward an outcome, which is especially useful if several factors are commonly selected.
- Learning from both wins and losses is equally important.
- Disengaged opportunities are often losses in disguise.
- Delayed deals, although still active, benefit from having win/loss reviews completed with the appropriate factors for delays.

NOTE

1. M. Khalsa and R. Illig, *Let's Get Real or Let's Not Play* (New York: Penguin Group, 2008). Reference is made to underscoring the advanced sales techniques of influencing the decision process and buying criteria; when these are known, there should be little doubt as to the factors affecting the final outcome.

CHAPTER 4

CAPTURING
THE DATA

The successful business is the one that finds out what is the matter with it before its competitors do.

—Business proverb

During the course of a sales engagement between a prospect and a seller, a myriad of factors come into play that affect the final outcome. Various sales models offer compelling cases and differing approaches for model effectiveness. The proliferation of sales models signals that there are probably several valid ways of organizing and parsing the sales process into neatly ordered stages in sequential or circular models, usually built around the customer at the center. However, the one stage that is conspicuously absent from almost every model, and arguably the most neglected, is the post-opportunity outcome review, or win/loss review.

Now that the deal has been won or lost, the information generated at the various sales stages has nowhere to go, no leverage to get to the next stage, and no apparent future value. The opportunity for leveraging the insights gained about this customer during the sales cycle breaks down at this point, but the information is still there—somewhere. Perhaps it is carefully documented in the CRM, artfully captured in a PowerPoint slide deck, calculated in a spreadsheet on a laptop hard drive, filed in a string of lengthy email conversations, or handwritten on a paper notepad from the numerous customer and partner encounters. It is also likely that information resides with more than one person and in more than one supporting system.

If yours is like many companies, you may have a rudimentary system for managing your opportunity pipeline. Perhaps it is an offline solution such as a document form, a personal spreadsheet template, or a robust customer relationship management (CRM) package. Some CRM systems provide a field that allows the account team to specify a loss reason when an opportunity is lost, but may not allow for capture of win factors.

UNLOCKING TACIT KNOWLEDGE

More often, however, a lot of *tacit* knowledge is sitting inside the seller's head. We earlier discussed how depending too heavily on good personal relationships could mask weaknesses that increase your business risks. Another risk associated with an overreliance on personal relationships is that information will stay with the seller if she moves into another position or leaves the company altogether. To emphasize this point, consider that the average attrition, or *churn,* rate for the sales profession in a large company is between 5% and 10%, taking into account natural and forced attrition. Imagine the hypothetical scenario that 5% to 10% of your CRM data is lost each year for various reasons (e.g., mismanaged

Think of the potential effects on your business if 10% of your data disappears from your organization each year along with your people!

data warehouses, disasters, security breaches, data vandalism, etc.). Your business would likely struggle to survive, if it was even able to reach profitability to begin with. Think of the potential effects on your business if 10% of your data disappears from your organization each year along with your people!

How, then, do we begin to harness, recycle, and manage this information and turn it into knowledge usable by a broad set of stakeholders? The process of transforming a seller's tacit knowledge into explicit or specifiable knowledge is known as *codification* or *articulation*. The key to codifying a large part of this tacit knowledge is to capture it with each transaction over time and in a concise format that can be analyzed and referenced by others.

With a structured framework to organize thought and combine tacit knowledge with discrete data, one begins to assemble information in such a way that new connections between seemingly disparate pieces of data begin to create knowledge. This assembly can be further enhanced by the use of information technology that further facilitates the capture, organization, and visualization of the insights.

Whatever the system used, it is important that the key factors leading to the outcome be captured in a timely manner, by the people closest to the action (typically the account manager or a team specialist), and with enough accurate information to enable the insights to develop and to guide future sales strategy and tactics.

There are four basic types of information that need to be captured during the win/loss review:

1. Opportunity details (discrete data)
2. Outcome factors (informed selection)
3. Narrative and opinion (tacit knowledge)
4. Negotiation tactics (learned skills)

Win/Loss Review—Data Entry Form				
Opportunity Details	**Outcome Factors**			
Customer:	**Offering**	**Relationship**	**Competitiveness**	**Services**
Opportunity Name:	❏ Factor 1	❏ Factor 1	❏ Factor 1	❏ Factor 1
Partner:	❏ Factor 2	❏ Factor 2	❏ Factor 2	❏ Factor 2
Competitor:	❏ Factor 3	❏ Factor 3	❏ Factor 3	❏ Factor 3
Deal Amount:	❏ Factor 4	❏ Factor 4	❏ Factor 4	❏ Factor 4
Outcome:				
Deal Summary	**Challenges Faced**		**Overcoming the Challenges**	
Narrative text	*Narrative text*		*Narrative text*	
Negotiation Tactics	*Narrative text*			

FIGURE 4.1   Sample Win/Loss Review Capture Form

The depth and breadth of each of these information types depend on several variables. Figure 4.1 represents a sample win/loss form for seller-generated win/loss reviews. The actual form should be software enabled to facilitate the capture, aggregation, reporting, and analysis in a more efficient and insightful way. Better still is for the process to be fully integrated into your CRM platform and part of your sales process rhythm.

OPPORTUNITY DETAILS

When designing the data structures for win/loss reviews, one should consider how the information will be used by others. There are a few attributes about an opportunity that need to be part of the win/loss record in order to enable BI capabilities. Simple details such as the outcome, competitors, product name, product version, date of sale (or loss), geography, industry, and partners may be all that is necessary to guide future searches and relevant basic insights. These attributes are also quite factual and objective, so there is little room to misinterpret their meanings. This base-level information should be drawn directly from a CRM or order entry platform where the data already exists to eliminate repetitive data entry.

If the win/loss review process is directly integrated into a CRM platform, then having all opportunity details can be useful as there may be some users or stakeholders who require some seemingly obscure data to complete their analysis. This is especially true for complex products or solutions that may actually be composed of hundreds of attributes. Full integration or the capability to pull those details is desirable even if most of the opportunity details will not be immediately used.

With an adequate number of transactions, trending information by product can be readily surfaced, for example. Further views of that factor in geography and industry can allow for simple comparative analysis. With the use of statistical tools such as Minitab®, one can draw correlations between different attributes using scatter diagrams and test for different hypotheses. However, this level of analysis usually falls outside of the domain of the sales teams.

OUTCOME FACTORS

To give meaning and context to the discrete opportunity data, understanding the forces exerted on the sales outcome falls uniquely within the domain of the sales teams. From prospect to close, and at every stage in between, the sales teams are exposed to dynamics and nuances from their customer interactions that few other groups in their company will know.

Most sellers know that there are several factors that lead to a particular outcome of an opportunity. Depending on the industry, there likely exists a known set of factors, beginning with factors that are common to nearly every customer engagement and sales transaction (e.g., price, product, relationship, services, etc.). Understanding which factors actually contribute to and have the greatest effect on the outcome depends on the skills of the sales teams. Ultimately, selection of these factors will be based on the presence of actual evidence, general perception and tacit knowledge, level of business acumen, and self-discipline.

Evidence of these factors can be found in many areas. Some evidence is factual and well documented (e.g., award letters, email notices, press releases), while others are more anecdotal in nature (e.g., informal or off-the-record customer discussions, competitive responses, knowledge of customer decision-making process).

The outcome factors can be grouped into general categories. For purposes of this illustration, we will use factors and categories commonly found in business. Remember, these factors need to be relevant to the industry in which you work, with some adjustments made to account for nuances in the industries or verticals you sell into.

Offering Factors

These factors relate to the actual offering, such as the product features, alignment with the customer needs, price/value proposition, and the strength of the solution. The offering is also where you are likely to find documented evidence that supports your conclusions. For example, a customer award letter might actually indicate what contributed to your win. In other cases, discussions with business or technical decision makers might reveal that there were some product features, or absence of them, that contributed to the outcome.

During the win/loss review process, selecting one or more of the offering factors might be an obvious choice, since without the offering there would be no opportunity. However, it is still important to understand whether and how much the factors around the offer contributed to the outcome relative to the factors in the other categories. Examples of offering factors might include:

- Product features
- Price/value proposition
- Total cost of ownership
- Solution alignment with customer needs

Relationship Factors

There's an old saying that "we buy from people we like and trust." The essence of this axiom is that one should not underestimate the impact that relationships have on business outcomes. At one level, this refers to the business-to-business, or organizational, relationship that one entity has with another. If the overall business relationship is longstanding and healthy, personnel changes within either company are likely to have less impact on the nature of the relationship.

On another level, there are the personal relationships that people have with individual members of the customer organization. Often, deals are won on the strength of positive relationships, even though the offering might not have been the most compelling one. The opposite can also be true: Sour relationships can negate even the most competitive of offerings.

When reviewing factors in this category, one must be clear as to whether the relationship factors are organizational in nature, personal, or both. For example, the phrase "relationship health" is typically used to refer to the organization and not the individual. This is important for correlating opportunity outcomes with specific elements in a customer satisfaction survey.

Examples of relationship factors include:

- Account management
- Business decision-maker relationships

- Technology decision-maker relationships
- Political alignment
- Corporate relationship health

Competitive Factors

Buying decisions are often made based on how well a solution and its value are differentiated from the competition and whether there are references and additional evidence to support a particular selection. All else being equal, the customer will lean toward an incumbent supplier if the key differentiator is that they already have internal skills to support the solution, which shortens the learning curve and reduces pains of switching vendors and platforms. For customers who are risk averse, having key customer references lined up might be the competitive differentiator that leads to the win. However, the opposite outcome might happen if you were unable to provide your customer with solid references of early adopters of a new product line.

Examples of competitive factors include:

- Customer evidence
- Reference customers available
- Differentiated competitive solution
- Incumbent supplier
- Internal IT skills

Service Factors

Service-related capabilities such as design, consulting, and support are distinguished from product sales. In some cases, services are perceived as the value-add components of a product sale. However, services may be *the* primary offering, in which case more detailed aspects about your service offering come into play. Lingering customer perceptions are likely influenced by past experiences with your direct services organization, or with your authorized channel. This works both for and against you and any engagement where services are offered should take a close look at prior deals to mitigate risks and leverage satisfaction from past customer interactions. If your professional services are related to mission-critical IT applications, customers will look closely at the strength of your support services (i.e., availability, service-level agreements [SLAs], severity escalation, onsite support, and channel expertise).

Services may also include your partner or intermediary channel. A customer's previous experience with a partner, or your partner's market position and experience with your product/solution, could be the differentiator in a sale.

Examples of service factors include:

- Partner expertise
- Customer experience with partner
- Partner availability
- Strength of service/support offering
- Past experience with service/support organization

Negotiation Tactics

A less known (and even less reviewed) area of understanding opportunity outcomes is what negotiation tactics were employed leading up to the final outcome. Deals are often won or lost on the strength of your negotiating skills. Negotiations are the activities commonly understood to occur toward the end of a sales cycle where the final give-and-take happens, or the terms and conditions are being finalized. This is often the case, and few can be faulted for viewing negotiations as a last-mile sales activity. In reality, real negotiations should begin when an opportunity enters your pipeline, where you create more leverage and a stronger bargaining position.

There is a commonly held belief that negotiation is a random set of verbal tactics that are based on soft communication skills. If one accepts this diagnosis, then the prescription is long lists of verbal countermeasures designed to be the antidote for virtually any negotiation. Research shows that verbal tactics act as anchors in negotiation, points around which negotiations may revolve. Requests for proposal (RFPs) sent out, first offers, legacy practices in the market, and, most important, words uttered all tend to anchor a negotiation.[1]

Opening offers in negotiations tend to have more impact on final outcomes than all subsequent offers combined. Think of a scenario where an account manager has labored for months on a $20 million deal, and she has learned that it is now her business to lose. The buyer says, "Congratulations, you've won the business, but your competitor offers pretty much the same thing and has dropped 10% below you, so you'll need to do better!" What typically happens? The account manager comes back to corporate and asks for a 12% discount to win the business. This decision has just cost your firm $2.4 million.

In another example, a buyer says to a sales representative, "You need to add in that higher level of services for free!" Say this is a $1.5 million deal and the cost of service enhancement is $5,500. Out of frustration (and perhaps a bit of ego) the account manager walks away from the deal and loses out on $1.5 million for one-third of 1%. Was this decision the right one? The answer is: "It depends."

It is important to consider the combined financial impact of these decisions over the course of a year in perhaps thousands of deals across the globe. This doesn't even take into consideration the impact on your brand equity of either playing hardball and losing or rolling over and winning.

The fact remains that these anchors influenced both wins and losses. Can we use feedback from salespeople about buyer tactics to assist here? The answer is *absolutely!* The information on the customer tactics used during previous engagements, which is captured by the win/loss reviews, helps sales teams anticipate what is likely to be said at the negotiation table. Armed with this knowledge, will your sales team be able to improve win rates without giving away the store? Our experience clearly shows that it will.

Customers are becoming much savvier about your own negotiation headroom well in advance of your first offer. Customers often retain the services of consultancies that specialize in specific supplier negotiations, and are using this information to their advantage. They are benefiting from the knowledge of hundreds or thousands of prior negotiations, perhaps with your own company. Unless a supplier company is doing its part to build its knowledge base of how deals are being negotiated with its target customers, it is at a distinct disadvantage.

CASE STUDY: PREDICTING NEGOTIATIONS

Think! Inc., a negotiation consultancy founded by a Harvard Business School professor and member of the executive board for the Harvard negotiation project, studied verbal negotiating tactics from buyers over a three-year period in 19 countries, among a wide range of Fortune 500 companies in many industries.*

This study was done to discover whether these tactics followed any kind of predictable pattern or whether negotiation is truly as random and unpredictable as most companies think. The reality astounded them: 97% of verbal tactics used by buyers globally followed two very predictable patterns:

1. The buyer referenced an alternative to your company.
2. The buyer used that alternative as leverage for a concession.

---

*Think! Inc., a Chicago-based negotiation consultancy. Study adapted by permission from Brian Dietmeyer, President of Think! Inc.

(continued)

The buyer's most common approach was to combine both:

- "Your competition is so much more flexible than you are."
- "You are way out of line with the market."
- "Everyone else gives that away for free."
- "Your service and reliability are lower than your competitors'"

The second most common approach was simply to ask for a concession:

- "Lower your price."
- "Sharpen your pencil."
- "It's not in my budget."
- "Congratulations—you've won the business. Now give me 10% less."

The words are different but the pattern remains the same. The most common negotiation tactic in the world is: "I can get the same thing cheaper." This tactic combines both the alternative and concession tactics and is probably costing you millions when it shouldn't. Seasoned account managers are still rocked back on their heels when faced with these tactics.

These tactics follow a pattern that is probably exactly the same in your company. If we collect the most common or most difficult buyer verbal tactics from win/loss reviews, there are several ways to use this data. We can learn from wins and losses, determining where we caved in to concession pressure needlessly to win the business, or where we succeeded or failed in neutralizing buyer tactics.

More importantly, we can:

- Anticipate what is likely to happen at the closing table
- Be prepared with objective counter data on "same thing" and "cheaper"
- Recognize that, while the words may be different, customers are following a pattern
- Be a more effective negotiator

Other Categories

The four previously discussed categories of opportunity factors are likely to cover about 90% of the key factors leading to the deal outcome in most industries. There are several other factors that, depending on the industry, can be grouped in the "other" category. Mergers and acquisitions, regulatory issues, industry innovations, and so forth are factors that may not fit neatly in the preceding four categories, but are just as influential as the other factors. When reported in aggregate, these factors can uncover developing market forces and risks that influence sales outcomes, which can be either exploited or mitigated.

The "other" factor category is also your opportunity to discover factors you may not be aware of. By adding the "other" category and providing the ability for the sales team to enter their own factors, you can analyze these over time to see whether there are emerging trends or other reasons you are winning deals that are outside of your current understanding.

Examples of other factors include:

- Merger or acquisition
- Regulatory environment
- External political climate

THE NARRATIVE

Perhaps the most subjective section of the win/loss process, but the one containing the most immediately actionable insights, is the narrative section. The seller analysis contains three subsections that briefly summarize the nature of the deal, the key challenges faced, and how the challenges were faced (for wins) or might have been overcome (for losses). At the deal level, these are nuggets that sellers can learn from and apply to their current deal pipeline. In aggregate, these can reveal insights that can inform general sales strategy for sales managers, provide product feedback to product development and marketing teams, and reveal new and emerging competitive opportunities and threats for senior leadership.

The text need not be a dissertation. In fact, brevity (50 to 100 words for each part) is the key to facilitate the capture and the consumption of the information contained. The activity resembles the social media phenomenon of microblogs such as Twitter. Here, very quick capture of thoughts in crisp and concise nuggets is all that is needed to provide additional context to the factors selected. From the contribution side of the process, this is one of the key design principles that allow for sharing a maximum of insights while minimizing tax on selling time.

On the consumption side of the process, when sellers query the report database for information that will help them win a particular opportunity, there may be dozens or even hundreds of deal outcomes that can be browsed. Aside from making browsing and reading the narratives simpler for the seller, as we will discuss in Chapter 5, "Surfacing the Insights," aggregating the narratives into consumable summaries by internal subject matter experts will be greatly facilitated by keeping to relevant and concise insights.

If there is a need for further inquiry on a specific opportunity, the seller can contact the opportunity owner for more information.

- **Deal summary.** This section describes the opportunity at a very high level. This may contain information about what the customer is seeking, the solution proposed, and the competitive environment. It need not be very specific, and it should be brief. General information that is already known about an account or is already contained in an account plan should not be repeated here. Nor should this contain information that is not relevant to the deal.

- **Challenges faced.** This section focuses on the most significant challenges faced while managing the specific deal through its sales stages. These should support the opportunity factors selected in the prior section, but provide additional context. For example, the biggest challenge might have been a competitor's pricing, with the competitor practically giving away its product or solution as a loss leader. Another might have been the customer expectations regarding commitments to the delivery timeline, or customer perception of product performance compared with a competitor. Challenges can come from many sources, internal and external, from within or outside of your control, and at any time during the sales stage. It is important to stay relevant to the key challenges so that others can benefit from your insightful approaches in addressing these challenges, or benefit from your hindsight in the case of a loss. We have all been in situations where we have said, "If I could do it again, I would . . ."

- **Overcoming the challenges.** It is how we dealt with those challenges that provides golden insights for sales teams wishing to improve their chances of winning. Remember that these insights can come from both wins and losses. For wins, there may be several actions that are repeatable by other sellers. In really challenging situations it is sometimes tempting for sellers to attribute the overcoming of challenges to the heroic efforts of their teams (e.g., "Arranged an executive meeting between our president and customer CEO"); however, these solutions often are not scalable or readily available to the broader sales force. Nevertheless, they may offer approaches previously not considered. For losses, the insights come in the form of what might have been done differently to effect a favorable outcome (i.e., "If I could start over, I would . . ."). Sometimes it is only after a period of reflection on a loss that the remedies become clear. Better to let others benefit from your learnings.

ACCOMMODATING MULTIPLE LANGUAGES

English is often regarded as the *lingua franca* of international business. Still, multinational companies might wish to accommodate localized (i.e., multilanguage) interfaces and permit the narratives to be captured in their native tongue, ensuring that insights are not lost in translation. The opportunity details and the factors selected will be indexed along with all other entries and included in all analytical activities. This is made possible since the system design will have logic and service layers separate from the user interface layer.

Permitting native-language narratives lets individuals feel more comfortable when adding insights and benefit from being able to see and discover insights in their own language. While some additional investment may be required to professionally translate the narratives into a common language, the quantitative elements are language-neutral and universally roll up for central reporting and analysis without any additional translation. A more sophisticated system might permit filtering of reports and narratives in multiple languages.

In Chapter 5, we'll examine use-case scenarios of how the information contained in the data store can be turned into competitive insights. As our focus is on catering to the needs of front-line sellers, we will start with them and then progress toward how sales managers, product and marketing teams, and senior leadership might enjoy the fruits of the information provided by the sales teams.

SUMMARY

- Sales models rarely include win/loss reviews as an integral part of their sales stages.
- Information gathered during the course of a sales engagement resides in multiple locations and formats, and most often resides within the brains of account team members.

- Information technology offers a structured framework to organize thought and combine tacit knowledge with discrete data and converts this into easily consumed insights.
- Together, the opportunity details, outcome factors, narrative text, and negotiation tactics provide the four pillars that support the capture, reporting, and analysis of insights for use by a broad spectrum of stakeholders.
- The outcome factors are categorized by offerings, relationships, competitiveness, services, and negotiation. Other categories exist and depend on the industry. Factor selection is facilitated by predefined lists and often enhanced with compelling user interfaces.
- Capturing negotiation tactics during the win/loss reviews provides unique and predictive views of future negotiations. This helps the sales teams to anticipate and be better prepared to manage the negotiation anchors in future engagements.
- Brief narratives provide context to the structured data, provide the seller-to-seller dialogue, and highlight nuances of the transaction.
- Native-language capabilities allow for the original insights to be captured without being lost in translation. The structured data remains neutral as the services layer is separated from the application layer.

NOTE

1. D. Malhotra and M. Bezerman, *Negotiation Genius: How to Overcome Obstacles and Achieve Brilliant Results at the Bargaining Table and Beyond* (New York: Bantam Dell, 2007).

CHAPTER 5

SURFACING THE INSIGHTS

The purpose of computing is insight, not numbers.

—Richard Hamming

Surfacing and using the insights previously captured from the sales teams from the win/loss review process is indeed the essence of this book. Insights gained are where the stakeholders will begin to see the real value from the collective intelligence from field sales. Some insights will be in the form of the simple tactical details from previous opportunities won or lost, others may surface when analyzing trends, and still others will pop when more rigorous statistical and correlation tests are performed. This section deals with the methods used for searching for and analyzing vast quantities of information and drawing correlations among the various factors and outcomes. Later, we will also look at methods for deriving statistical correlations that provide stronger evidence and causal relationships between the factors and outcomes.

Needed to really apply insights are the outcome factors, accompanied by their short narratives, that led to the actual outcome.

SALES SCENARIO: USING WIN/LOSS REVIEW
DATA FOR ACTIVE OPPORTUNITIES

Steve is an account manager for a large multinational. His team is facing strong competition in a deal calling for a cloud-based customer relationship management (CRM) solution. Accessing the reporting feature of the win/loss review system using his browser, Steve searches for and creates a report of past deals, filtering on specific criteria such as the competitors involved and the industry to which this deal applies. He also looks at the deals where a specific partner was engaged.

By reviewing the outcomes of those past deals (wins and losses) and the factors that contributed to the outcome, Steve is able to apply specific and/or general insights to this deal. Insights provided by other sellers allowed Steve and his team to copy successful approaches and to avoid the tactical errors made by other teams that led to undesirable outcomes.

The benefits are enabled by conducting proper win/loss reviews to begin with, capturing and feeding this information into the win/loss review system, and making it accessible again to the sellers and the broader stakeholder community.

Accessing this information is critical to getting the right information to the seller at the right time. Ideally, the search tool should contain ways to match the opportunity attributes, and also the factors that led to the outcome. As you will recall, these factors are captured by the seller after the deal has been won or lost through the win/loss review. These outcome factors are where the *relevance* of the searches gets optimized. For example, finding past deals where political alignment was a primary factor might reveal additional insights into winning that may not have been thought of before. This could also have been the factor for some prior losses. You will recall from Chapter 3 that the factors for wins should be the same ones that could lead to a loss. The accompanying narratives will provide the additional anecdotal insights.

Any system that is well-designed and scaled to capture data will generate a lot of it. Some of this data is prepopulated from business systems (e.g., CRM, order processing, etc.). Perhaps the system is also normalized, meaning that the field attributes are fixed to contain only a certain type of data, or it may be binary (yes/no). It may also contain variable-length data fields that contain written text. With so much data and so many types of data it can be intimidating to try to distill the nuggets of information that can be reused at all levels of the organization, especially at the front line.

TACTICAL INSIGHTS

At times the information needed is tactical, time sensitive, and around a specific sales scenario. In this case, a seller may consult the search and reporting mechanism of the win/loss reviews, querying the database to reflect the attributes of the deal currently being attended to. It is important to note that we're referring to the entire database, not merely the records that this particular seller previously entered. Many well-intentioned, seller-oriented tools for conducting win/loss reviews are focused on providing sellers with their own reference library of insights from past opportunities. While these facilitate the review and reflection of the tactical behaviors and activities that the seller performed, the design is focused on individual sales practice improvement.

By taking a different approach, whereby learning and performance improvement are expected to be shared experiences, we start to realize the *multiplier effect* and the value of this

Knowledge becomes the currency that experiences the power of the multiplier effect.

information. Borrowing from a simple financial markets metaphor, let's assume that a bank receives $1,000 in new deposits. Assuming that the bank is required to keep 20% of deposits on reserve, it has $800 to lend to other customers. When the $800 is deposited into other banks, which are also subject to the 20% reserve requirement, each bank can now lend out $640. This continues until the original $1,000 turns into $5,000 in deposits! This creation of deposits is due to the multiplier effect. In an effective database, instead of money, knowledge is the currency that experiences the power of the multiplier effect.[1]

Supporting this notion are two of the core tenets of the win/loss review system described here: the *transparency* and *accessibility* of information. A seller in country A will benefit from the collective entries from all sellers in countries A, B, C, and so on. Very soon, the knowledge collected will provide a library of rich experiences to be shared and learned from.

To find insights that can be put into immediate use, the seller might elect to search on prior deals by a key word or string of words that contain unique values. For example, if a seller is looking for past deals in his system that have something do to with "London," there may be several hundred results for this search since "London" may be contained in the location, in the text narratives, in the name of the opportunity, or in the name of a competitor or a partner. Entering a more unique search term related to an opportunity, such as "hydraulic," may return more relevant opportunities that have something to do with hydraulic systems, but not necessarily those past opportunities in London or in the same industry as the opportunity that seller is pursuing.

Most databases and search engines today support Boolean-style searches. *Boolean* search techniques can be used to carry out effective searches to arrive at the relevant records related to a particular deal. Using Boolean logic to broaden or narrow the search for similar past deals is not as complicated as it sounds. It is likely that anyone familiar with a computer and the Internet is already using Boolean search techniques. Let's assume that you are working in the high-tech software industry, and the deal you are trying to close is for a client in the energy business. You also know that the company specializes in renewable energy sources. Consulting your win/loss database, your Boolean search string might be "energy AND renewable," or "green AND energy" (see Figure 5.1). In this case, you want to narrow down the search results to just the handful of past deals that contain both terms. Perhaps the results are too few, or the ones that you found were not useful. To increase the number of search results, you enter "energy OR renewable" or perhaps "green OR energy."

The search now returns quite a few more results, each record containing either the term "energy" or the term "green." With the previously described types of data fields, it is important to accommodate this search method, and that all fields, whether fixed or variable, be indexed and discoverable by Boolean logic searches.

Another search method involves displaying the available search fields and allowing the selection of single values by radio-button selectors, or multiple values through multi-select checkboxes. In this method, the search criteria are presented as items that the

Search Results for "Green" AND "Energy"	Search Results for "Green" OR "Energy"
1. Highland Plant **green energy** project 2. Smart **energy** grid for a **green** environment 3. **Green energy** power generation	1. Highland Plant **green energy** project 2. Smart **energy** grid for a **green** environment 3. **Green energy** power generation 4. **Energy** monitoring solution 5. BI solution for **green** initiative 6. CRM for Northeast **Energy** Association 7. Renewable **energy** system for ABC

FIGURE 5.1 How Search Operators Affect Search Results

Win/Loss Review–Search Tool

Enter search term			*Search*

Outcome	Competitor	Industry	Region
❏ Win	❏ Competitor 1	❏ Industry 1	❏ Region 1
❏ Loss	❏ Competitor 2	❏ Industry 2	❏ Region 2
❏ Disengage	❏ Competitor 3	❏ Industry 3	❏ Region 3
	❏ Competitor 4	❏ Industry 4	❏ Region 4
	❏ Competitor 5	❏ Industry 5	❏ Region 5
	❏ Competitor 6	❏ Industry 6	❏ Region 6

Relationship Factors	Competitive Factors	Services Factors
❏ Account Management	❏ Differentiated Solution	❏ Onsite Support
❏ Team Orchestration	❏ Customer References	❏ 24/7 Escalation
❏ Political Alignment	❏ Incumbent Supplier	❏ Maint. Agreement

FIGURE 5.2 Sample Win/Loss Review Search Form Template

user can select to filter the results. This uses the Boolean "AND" operator by default, meaning that as one selects more criteria, fewer results that match the selected criteria are displayed. Figure 5.2 provides an example of a simple search form that combines the use of a free-form text search bar and predefined search criteria enabled with checkboxes.

Considering that integrated and institutionalized win/loss review systems will potentially generate several thousand records, having predefined search criteria that improve result relevance is important for front-line sellers who cannot afford to spend a lot of time researching lengthy case studies.

The use-case scenarios that follow illustrate this point. Beginning with the front-line seller, let's consider a few use-case scenarios where sellers are likely to need some additional information to help them win opportunities they are managing.

**USE-CASE SCENARIOS FOR SURFACING INSIGHTS
FROM WIN/LOSS REVIEWS**

Scenario 1: John is working on the early stages of a competitive deal and wants to get a general sense of how his peers won against a particular competitor and to avoid some of the traps from lost deals. John searches the records for past opportunities won and lost against a specific competitor. John notices that in the majority of these wins, "Price/Value Proposition" was selected as a key factor, along with "Relationship Health." Where there were losses, John notices that "Price/Value Proposition" was also frequently selected, but that "Relationship Health" was not. Reading through the narratives, John was able to notice a trend toward executive engagement early in the sales cycle. John was able to secure early executive engagement from his senior executives, thereby helping to neutralize his competitor's advantage.

Scenario 2: Sue is working a competitive deal in an industry that is highly price sensitive and where it is expected that no one will have a price advantage. Sue turns to the win/loss reports and finds that most of the wins had the factor "24/7 and Onsite Critical Support" selected. Sue also noticed that most of the losses had the same factor selected. So it became clear that having this support contributed to the wins, while not having it was a significant factor for the losses. There did not seem to be any trends with a particular competitor. Further reviewing the narratives, Sue noticed that it was the emphasis on service and support factors that made the difference in outcomes in most cases. This provided Sue with insights as to the key differentiator against all other proposals, which she was able to proactively address within her company ahead of her proposal being due.

Scenario 3: Bill noticed that one of his major deals for a banking client was stuck in the later stages of the sales cycle. Any further delays increased the risk of losing the deal outright to the incumbent. Bill consulted the win/loss reports and queried the deals won in the banking industry against this particular competitor. Nearly all of the

(continued)

past deals won had "Product Features" checked and the narratives indicated that this particular competitor could not integrate with the client's CRM platform. Bill contacted a couple of the opportunity owners to confirm his findings. He also exploited this vulnerability and emphasized his solution's ability to integrate with the CRM in subsequent interactions. Prior to this, Bill was primarily emphasizing the strengths of his service and support offerings, something that was expected but not what the customer was looking for to move the purchase forward.

Running ad hoc reports that narrow in on the specifics of a particular deal can be an effective way to counter competitive threats and to learn from ideas previously tried. In the three previous scenarios, a seller consults the prior deals that most closely match the active deals currently being managed. Whether a simple database of prior deals on a large spreadsheet, or a more robust CRM platform that provides advanced search capabilities, the objective is the same: to find, learn, and apply the insights from past deals that are relevant to the active opportunity.

Some commercial CRM platforms build in rudimentary capabilities for matching deals with other deals so as to enable collaboration with other sales teams and share best practices. Most popular CRM packages, such as those from Microsoft, Oracle, SAP, and Salesforce.com, have customizable features that can accommodate opportunity outcome analytics and reporting. Some also have features that match deals based on similar characteristics of the opportunity. The deal is matched primarily around the usual details about the opportunity, which gives some general direction in which to look for additional information, such as the owners of the other opportunities. Attributes such as deal size, industry served, partners, and competitors involved can be matched in a meaningful way so as to improve relevance. However, additional attributes such as the opportunity factors are needed to *optimize* relevance.

STRATEGIC INSIGHTS

The strength of a broad stakeholder-oriented win/loss review process is its capability to inform beyond the immediate needs of a sales opportunity to sales strategy and to provide a strong bridge between sales and marketing.

When applied to sales strategy, win/loss reviews can supply valuable insights for account management frameworks, customer life-cycle management policies, partnership models, opportunity prospecting and qualification, and pipeline management. For example, say management reports reveal that losses in a particular geography against a competitor are increasing over the past three quarters. Cross-checking the information contained in the seller narratives and factors selected, it is concluded that your partner channel does not have the expertise to compete against this competitor. Further research shows that no one on your sales team has any subject matter expertise on these particular products. A strategy is then formulated to strengthen channel expertise by reallocating resources to build this sales capability. Although an individual seller might have felt the pain of the loss against this competitor, only the management team, through the aggregated intelligence provided by the sales teams, is able to determine the breadth and depth of this risk to the organization and convert the insights into a strategy.

In Chapter 3, "Why Do We Win or Lose?," we discussed disengaged opportunities as one of three usual outcomes of an opportunity. When we consider that from 50% to 70% of opportunities are disengaged or go into an inactive state, the win/loss review might point to issues related to, for example, opportunity qualification or sales operations. It might also reveal deficiencies within your own sales teams, which may not be capable of managing increasingly complex sales, preferring instead to walk away from certain deals. Using the latter example, our reports indicated that in the aerospace industry, there are a disproportionately high number of sales opportunities that have become inactive, or disengaged. Together, the value of these opportunities could easily retire your quota. However, your sales teams indicate as their reason for disengaging that they have a low probability of winning. They decide not to spend their energies pursuing the opportunity, preferring instead to spend their time on lower-hanging fruit. That may be a valid reason in many cases, but upon further investigation by your sales leadership, it is discovered that there are resources at your team's disposal that could have addressed the complexity and depth of the opportunity. Your company might have centralized competitive or industry resources that could have been called upon were they known to exist. The sales leadership also noticed this phenomenon occurring in the health-care and retail industries. They immediately go into action to ramp up industry-related consultative selling skills, and combined these with training on awareness and utilization of internal sales resources.

Sales teams become a part of marketing's global intelligence network. There is also considerable strategic benefit for marketing departments. Marketers are skilled at keeping their fingers on the pulse of what is going on with their customers and competitors in the larger market. There are a multitude of tools and techniques at their disposal that provide a broad array of customer feedback. Customer surveys, brand studies, primary and secondary research—all are powerful mechanisms for providing clarity around market position and to drive future development efforts. As is often the case, however, sales typically discourages marketing from directly interacting with their customer base without their consent.

Win/loss reviews act as an early warning system for the marketing teams around competitive initiatives previously undetected or unnoticed, in addition to providing a more real-time and continuous flow of insights from customer interactions. In essence, sales teams become a part of marketing's global intelligence network.

For example, when reviewing the win/loss reports pertaining to a specific product, marketing might have noticed the emergence of a competitive bundling strategy with a third-party competitor. Upon deeper analysis, the bundling strategy appeared isolated to a particular market, but because it appeared to be gaining a competitive advantage, it was suspected that a broader bundling campaign was soon to be announced on a national or global scale. This enabled marketing to act sooner than if they had discovered that a global campaign was already underway.

Win/loss reviews also serve as an important feedback loop to gauge the effectiveness of broader campaigns or programs designed to drive demand. Consider that marketing often produces customer case studies, customer references, playbooks, and a host of assorted materials that help sales teams. A marketing team would like to know which of these assets were the most effective in helping sales close business, and which ones were not at all effective. This knowledge allows the marketing team to refocus its efforts where there is most return on its marketing investments.

Having a win/loss review process that is designed to improve strategic alignment between sales and marketing, we see the detectable impact on their respective scorecards and key performance indicators (KPIs). Sales will enjoy the benefits of faster pipeline velocity and less friction in the sales cycle; the cost of goods sold decreases as efforts are streamlined and maximized for efficiency; and there are fewer competitive losses and more responsive and customer-driven product development efforts.

SUMMARIZING THE INFORMATION

As discussed earlier, an institutionalized win/loss review process will create vast amounts of data. Finding the relevant data and turning it into meaningful, actionable knowledge can be facilitated by powerful search, reporting, and analytical tools and methods available to a wide audience. Preempting this potential overload, the design of the capture form focuses on the relevant details, and the narratives are given character limits. This ensures that when the reports are viewed, users do not have to read through hundreds of short narratives, but can quickly scroll through the insights so as to paint a mental picture from them, if not use them as they are written. There may be additional benefit from summarizing the information into aggregated and more consumable summaries.

In some cases there may be just too much information to sift through to get to the top-value insights in an efficient way. Reports may provide a high degree of relevance, but the number of records to review may be more than a user wishes to go through. In addition, the summary information is useful for internal newsletters, competitive summary reports, and competitive highlights sections of the win/loss review tool itself. It can also be used in reports where a user is finding all records pertaining to a particular competitor, and where the results will first show this aggregated summary for that competitor. This might guide users looking for deeper insights from the specific win/loss review records themselves. Figure 5.3 illustrates this point with a highly simplified example.

To summarize this information, one might consider soliciting the services of internal or external competitive intelligence (CI) experts to focus on the data where they can summarize the insights for general consumption. These summaries may not provide the granularity of insights or tactics used in specific sales scenarios, but they can be extremely useful in guiding competitive strategy.

Let's assume that you are working in an industry where there are four or five primary competitors. For Competitor A, a person or department with knowledge about this competitor can review the uncondensed insights coming from the field, analyze the data, draw correlations, and publish their guidance in summary form about how to compete against Competitor A. Guidance about

Non-Aggregated Narratives	Aggregated and Summarized Format
(Loss) Did not have a strong partner presence or expertise. Need to source new partner from other area.	
(Win) Customer indicated that visit from VP was very well received and convinced CEO of our vision.	Seller experiences suggest having strong partners combined with executive-level engagements. Exploit their weak product road map and lack of CRM support.
(Win) In final presentation we emphasized areas of our road map that we knew ACME didn't have without directly mentioning them.	
(Win) We demonstrated how our platform could integrate with their existing CRM, eliminating the need for them to invest in a new CRM.	

FIGURE 5.3   Summarizing Win/Loss Review Verbatims about a Specific Competitor

Competitors B, C, and D will surface in similar fashion. General guidance can also surface around the particular industries and partners involved.

ACCOUNTABILITY FOR SURFACING INSIGHTS

To surface the insights into broadly usable form, we'll focus on three widely used methods: internal, third-party facilitated, and volunteer subject matter experts.

An internal framework for analyzing and surfacing valuable insights is a very effective method for closing the loop among a broad set of stakeholders. A company may have a staff of CI experts trained on analyzing specific competitive strengths and weaknesses. Their accountabilities usually include keeping informed on competitive offerings and strategies, and communicating competitive market trends to sales and marketing departments. The information from seller-generated win/loss reviews is often a welcome information source for these experts, especially if it comes with analytical tools that help them build their own insights. Perhaps the competitive experts are seated within a specific industry or vertical organization.

A distinct advantage of this internal method is that the CI experts are more capable of detecting the nuances and hidden meanings embedded within the field-generated intelligence. Having focused on specific competitors allows them to place the data and narratives in context.

In the rapidly growing CI profession, many consultancies specializing in CI are finding brisk business in helping their companies understand their competitors. Some specialize in analyzing information that is already captured by their customer, while others offer more complete services—from conducting direct customer interviews to preparing the final reports. Consultancies will have the expertise in analyzing data and drawing insights. They will also bring a certain objectivity to the process, but may not have the market-knowledge intimacy that enables in-house CI experts to detect subtle clues that could influence the relevancy of the insights.

In cases where a company is working with a CI consultancy, there are some concerns with farming out highly sensitive information to a third party. That sensitivity is not merely confined to the fact that competitive strengths and weaknesses are being shared outside the company; there may be liabilities for information leaked that may contain inflammatory remarks about competitors. Information leaks can cause irreversible damage to a company's image and competitive strategy, not to mention the legal liabilities they may carry. Still, most reputable CI consultancies operate under very high professional standards and a strict ethical code. Professional organizations such as the Strategic and Competitive Intelligence Professionals promote and uphold a high ethical standard among their members and throughout the CI profession.

There is also a middle ground of sorts, whereby a company outsources its CI analysis, but, before turning over the data, sanitizes it of any sensitive information that directly identifies the competitor, customer, and account team names. These will be replaced with temporary placeholder names that can then be mapped back to the actual names once the analysis is safely back inside company borders. For example, ACME Computers might be designated as "Company A."

Perhaps your company does not have the breadth and depth of CI analysts to perform analysis to this level of sophistication, or the budget to outsource this activity to a third party. General guidance can still be surfaced with a disciplined review of the data, perhaps by willing members in the sales and marketing teams who are passionate about a particular competitor, or who may be recruited to take on the activity as a career development exercise.

What a company does with the insights gained from the win/loss review process of course depends on what is learned, what the goals are, and who is taking the action. Sales teams will take different actions than those of the product groups and senior leaders. The point here is that the information must trigger some form of action that leverages the knowledge gained. As we are trying to optimize competitive performance, as long as there are losses in our outcomes, it is safe to assume that some actions are expected.

Some insights may be as simple as probing for some repeated or common tactical activities that were part of past wins against a particular competitor. In these instances, action plans for a particular account or opportunity can be updated to reflect these useful tactics.

Not all insights may be explicit. For example, the narratives contained in win/loss reviews from past deals could surface potential new business opportunities that were previously not considered with a particular customer. These may guide sales managers to coach their teams during "whitespace" business development discussions.

TRENDS AND STATISTICAL EVIDENCE

There are many insights to be gained from browsing through the report results and narratives and by reviewing the business intelligence graphs and other visualization techniques. A common analytical technique is to view performance trends over time, enabled by compelling graphics. Here, one may quickly spot the upward or downward movement of a KPI. Trends alone may not necessarily reveal actionable insights, but they do point to areas that may be fertile for taking corrective action. For example, in reviewing the win rates over a particular time period against a specific competitor, you notice that the win rates relative to the losses are steadily decreasing. But you also notice that the total *number of opportunities* engaged against this particular competitor is increasing. So a decreasing win rate during a period of increased pipeline activity is certainly worrisome. This may indicate product or channel issues, or perhaps it reflects more unqualified opportunities entering the pipeline, which lead to higher loss and disengaged rates. Further investigation revealed that the losses were prevalent when a particular partner was involved in the deal. When the data was reviewed without the deals where this partner was engaged, the win rates were actually trending upward. This pointed to a deeper review of the partner capabilities in representing your product line. It also informed the channel leadership that partner diversification or specialization may help mitigate risks in the market from relying too closely on too few channel partners.

While the visual and anecdotal evidence suggests that there may be an identified factor that is affecting the outcome of opportunities over time, a rigorous statistical analysis can confirm the suspected causes. The theory developed to help explain the conditions is referred to as a *hypothesis.*

There are several statistical tools we can use to perform statistical analyses. One of the easiest tools to understand is the *Pareto chart.* This allows us to look quickly at each factor's relative contribution to the performance outcomes. In the example illustrated in Figure 5.4, we have graphed the frequency of the factors, expressed as a percentage, on why we are losing deals.

In this example, the revelation that *regulatory issues* was a significant factor was quite a surprise, especially since it was not previously suspected as a factor for losses. When the field inputs were aggregated and analyzed, this emerged as the primary factor for the losses. This then pointed to other factors, such as product specification compliance (not necessarily features), supplier registration status in a particular county, or several other

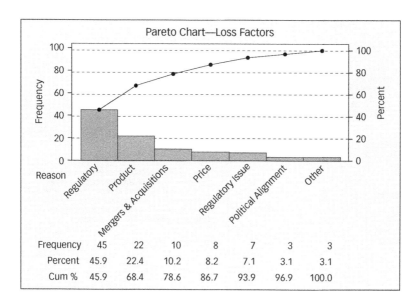

FIGURE 5.4 Pareto Chart Showing Relative Factor Contributions

regulatory issues that disqualified the product or solution from being considered.

In another scenario, your preliminary analysis pointed to a particular partner having higher win rates than most others. This is important to verify since you are going after a major deal and want to maximize your probability of winning. When selecting a partner to work with, your team recommended Partner A for the task. But since you wanted proof, you asked your Six Sigma Black Belt to perform an analysis to validate the recommendation. He recommended performing a Chi–Square hypothesis test, which is used to compare proportions against each other to decide whether there is statistical difference. The Chi–Square test was used to test whether Partner A was indeed more successful at winning over the other available partners. The results are shown in Figure 5.5.

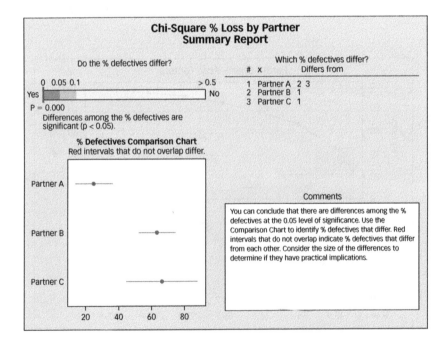

FIGURE 5.5   Chi-Square Test Comparing Proportion of Losses Expressed as Percentage Defectives

Since we are measuring percentage defectives, this analysis looks at the proportion of losses by partners. You concluded that there was strong statistical evidence to support your assertion that going with Partner A would maximize your chance of winning the deal.

SUMMARY

- Finding and using the insights previously captured from the sales teams from the win/loss review process realizes the value of the collective intelligence from field sales.
- Providing the capability to select opportunity attributes increases the relevance of the search results.
- A robust capture system will contain a mix of fixed and variable field data, including brief text narratives.
- Tactical insights are most commonly used by the sales teams with their active opportunities and are derived directly from the reporting mechanism.
- Democratizing the information has a multiplier effect, whereby the original value of the information is amplified as it is shared across the organization.
- A broad stakeholder-oriented win/loss review program can inform sales strategy and provide a strong bridge between sales and marketing.
- Trending analysis can reveal emerging competitive threats, channel vulnerabilities, and organizational deficiencies.
- Win/loss reviews also serve as an important feedback loop to gauge the effectiveness of broader campaigns or programs designed to drive demand.
- An institutionalized win/loss review process will create vast amounts of data, requiring efficient ways of finding, reviewing, and summarizing the insights.
- Insight analysis can be accomplished by in-house CI professionals, consultancies, or domain subject matter experts.

(continued)

- Trends alone do not necessarily reveal actionable insights, but they do point to areas that may be fertile for taking corrective action.
- There are various statistical tools and methods available to validate suspected areas of weakness and to uncover previously unforeseen factors that contribute to performance outcomes.

NOTE

1. The comparison with the banking industry is suitable because as the information is shared, it appears to multiply itself but at a decreasing intensity from its original form the farther it gets from its source.

CHAPTER 6

BEYOND COMPETITIVE INSIGHTS

Wisdom is the power that enables us to use knowledge for the benefit of ourselves and others.

—Thomas J. Watson

Win/loss reviews can be used to gain more than business and competitive insights. Architecting a win/loss review process using the design principles of a business intelligence platform will ensure that information can be recycled into many uses. You will recall that in Chapter 2, we introduced the paradigm "capture once, use often." The information captured can be easily repurposed for other activities, driving greater alignment and process efficiencies among sales, marketing, and operations. In the case of wins, these can form the base layer of an information store that can then feed into a process for recognizing key wins, nomination of sales awards, and the formation of customer evidence and case studies. Another advantage to achieving this integration with recognition, rewards, and case

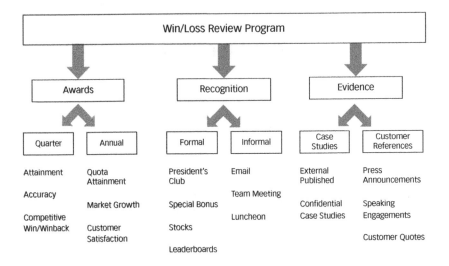

FIGURE 6.1 Win/Loss Reviews Serve as Entry Points to Other Programs

study development processes is that it reinforces the behavior of capturing the insights and key learnings of the outcome using the win/loss review process. It also sets the expectation that there is always something the sellers need to contribute by sharing their formula for success.

The strategy is to maximize the capture of field insights at every possible opportunity by integrating these programs with a win/loss review program. Figure 6.1 conceptualizes the win/loss review program as the entry point for awards, recognition, and evidence programs.

For employee recognition, a company may use various formal or informal processes to recognize and even reward key wins. At the most basic level, the ubiquitous email announcing a key win is something that most people are quite familiar with. Unfortunately, the information contained in these emails is not stored in a usable format or indexed in a manner by which it can be later searched for and referenced in a meaningful way. The amount of energy expended in crafting one of these email announcements is quite large, typically motivated by the prospect of widespread recognition by teams, peers, and leadership.

Now, imagine a way to harness the insights while preserving the celebratory nature of these recognition emails. The win/loss review process should be the starting point, and then built-in functionality within the tool can trigger the pull-through of the critical deal information into an email announcement template, with additional freeform text space to provide color commentary and acknowledgment of contributing members and senior leadership.

Going a step further, wins are often good candidates for award nominations in various categories. Many companies have a process to submit nominations for their respective periodic awards. The processes to initiate an award nomination are remark-

The strategy is to maximize the capture of field insights at every possible opportunity.

ably close to what one might find in a win/loss review process. Again, the difference is that the information captured usually remains within the domain of the awards program and is neither accessible nor reportable in a meaningful way to the numerous stakeholders who can use the insights toward future opportunities.

For the management teams in sales and marketing, the process of identifying wins that are worthy of broader public praise is made easier as the information is normalized, making big or strategic wins easier to identify. An added benefit of integrating rewards and recognition processes into an overall win/loss review process is that all of the emails and award nominations can later be referenced as artifacts within the win/loss review process, making them accessible to teams querying the database.

What nearly all of these programs have in common is that someone is documenting the reasons, or factors, that allow another person or team to evaluate the merits of the nomination. There is often some established guidance that those nominating people for the awards will follow to document the critical elements of the win and maximize the chances of their candidates winning the award. The components often follow the framework of a win/loss review process; there are the known details of the opportunity, the factors that contributed to the outcome, and the supporting narratives. Even less formal recognition activities, such as a broad email announcing a significant win, contain similar elements of the framework.

Insights from losses can also be used to provide critical insights to the product marketing and competitive intelligence teams. In these cases, the win/loss reviews can feed into the documentation process for competitive losses or for product improvement.

AWARD PROGRAMS

In most sales organizations there are usually several formal and informal programs for rewarding and recognizing team or individual performance. Some of these programs are short term and ad hoc, while others might have an established rhythm such as on a monthly, quarterly, or annual basis. The nominations are often facilitated by an online submission form or an offline document.

Quarterly award programs are usually designed to keep sales and marketing teams motivated throughout the fiscal year. By offering awards on an ongoing basis, individuals and teams are called out for various noteworthy achievements in performance. In sales, these may relate to sales forecast accuracy, forecast over-achievement, and competitive wins and winbacks. Annual awards often focus on quota achievement, major competitive wins, customer satisfaction, and market share growth.

When integrated with win/loss reviews, the initial information captured can strengthen the quality of the quarterly and annual awards submission, as well as the quantity. Award nominations with the highest chances of winning are those that are fact-based and document specific achievements, not just general statements. This information is already contained within the win/loss reviews.

Senior leaders often struggle to maintain quality consistency for frequently recurring award programs. Before they know it, the time has come again to reward their teams for outstanding performance, but what should be a pleasurable experience becomes a chore. And in an effort to find candidates, they must scramble their direct reports to find suitable candidates to reward. This often leads to rushed candidate submissions and inconsistent application of the award. The integrated win/loss review process provides the ready candidates, who can be quickly reviewed and narrowed to a short-list of candidates. And if the awards are stored and indexed in such a way that they become linked artifacts with the opportunity, they can also be referenced by others to see how the opportunity led to an award. And tracking awards becomes more simplified since the reporting process that allows filters of artifacts will quickly reveal prior awards.

The important point here is that any win/loss review process should be tied in with the processes you might already employ for recognizing key wins in your organization. If you show sellers a path to recognition for their efforts in conducting a win/loss review, they are more likely to see "what's in it for me." Of course, not all wins reviewed will guarantee broader recognition; however, having a review as a prerequisite will further encourage the expected behavior.

RECOGNITION

In addition to the formal award programs, recognition also plays an important part in any role. While award and recognition programs are often referred to interchangeably, we draw the distinction here to emphasize the psychological component of being recognized among peers and for the visibility to senior leadership. In sales and marketing, recognition programs range from the informal "pat on the back" for a job well done to the more formal "President's Club," typically the most prestigious recognition bestowed in sales and marketing at a major enterprise. Recognizing strong sales performance on an ongoing basis is a core element for sales motivation. To support this there are typically several ongoing programs to recognize outstanding sales performance.

The most common recognition method is the informal congratulatory emails announcing a major or significant win. These are known by many names—winwires, kudos, or win announcements. Email win announcements can bring great benefits by integrating with the win/loss review process. Similar benefits as with the award integration can be realized since much of the information is already captured in the win/loss reviews. What remains to be added is the commentary to support the noteworthy win. Additional information such as the supporting members and executive support can be added at this point.

In addition to the informal recognition activities, there are the formal programs, which are more structured and typically include some monetary compensation. Sellers are often incentivized to exceed performance targets with various sales contests and campaigns. Often the product marketing teams will announce special incentives, or "spiffs," to stimulate specific product sales. For these formal recognition programs, there is an opportunity to operationalize and integrate the process so that while someone or some team is getting formally recognized, the person or group is first leaving behind the critical insights of the deal that can also be used in the win/loss reports and analytics. The nomination programs for President's Club, special bonuses and stock, and leaderboards can also begin with the requirement that their nominations are sourced from the win/loss review program.

MARKETING CASE STUDIES

In many companies, marketing is tasked with creating external case studies and customer references from successful sales engagements. Case studies are indispensable artifacts that strengthen the credibility of a company's solutions to meet customer demands. As noted in Chapter 4, "Capturing the Data," the presence or absence of solid customer references can be one of the critical factors in the "competitive" category that sway customer decisions.

From where do the marketers obtain their case study leads or source their key win information? Often, this is done through informal internal channels, sales reports, internal newsletters, and the ad hoc email win announcement. It often depends upon someone initiating an action such as forwarding an email or manually sifting through various internal websites or information stores to source good case study candidates.

As illustrated in Figure 6.2, a standardized win/loss review process can provide both the base information and the research function needed to originate the efficient development of these case studies. Each layer in the model informs the succeeding layer with reusable information. As outlined in the previous section, these case studies can then also be available as linked artifacts within the win/loss review reporting process.

Similar to win/loss reviews, customer case studies are usually based on a single sales event, such as a solution sale. They usually provide an in-depth description of the event and explore the factors leading to the successful outcome. In many companies, case studies follow a template for collecting and presenting the information in a uniform way. The process of generating the case studies is useful in itself as it enables a deeper examination of what led to the outcome.

Since case studies are usually quite detailed and lengthy and have a marketing orientation, they are often conducted by marketing

FIGURE 6.2 Win/Loss Review Value Chain

or perhaps outsourced to an agency that specializes in producing these important artifacts. During the assembly of the case study, marketing will often consult with sales and services to gather the evidence needed. Integrated win/loss reviews already completed by sales can provide the base layer of evidence, allowing the case study authors to focus more on the value messaging instead of spending time on the tactical information that has already been captured.

Like award candidates, finding candidates for case studies can be facilitated by the search engine for win/loss reviews. For example, a product team wishing to increase its case studies for solutions that include specific products in a specific industry may easily find candidates in the win/loss review reports. Perhaps the cases needed are for internal purposes that focus on unique product or outlier solution sets that need further documentation. This may be useful for teams that specialize in incubating new and emerging products where there may not yet be critical mass. In this case, consulting the win/loss reviews for both wins and losses will provide these teams with new candidates for further study.

Upon reading the narratives, those searching for new case study candidates can then contact the opportunity owner to further inquire as to the viability of the solution as a case study. Of course, other important steps such as securing the customer's consent will be needed. The point here is that case selection can be made much more efficient while the viable pool of candidates for case development is greatly expanded.

SUMMARY

- A win/loss review process can be designed to recycle the information captured into many uses beyond analyzing performance and competitive intelligence.
- The information captured can be easily repurposed for other activities, driving greater alignment and process efficiencies among sales, marketing, and operations.
- Wins can form the base layer of an information store that can then feed into a process for recognizing key wins, nomination of sales awards, and the formation of customer evidence and case studies.
- A company may employ various formal or informal processes to recognize and even reward key wins, although not always in a reusable format.

CHAPTER 7

MEASURING PROCESS AND OUTCOME PERFORMANCE

One of the most important tasks of a manager is to eliminate his people's excuses for failure.

—Robert Townsend

An effective win/loss review process includes the capability for measuring the contributions of specific factors toward opportunity outcomes, but also the performance of the process itself. This includes measuring its broad scale adoption against predetermined or baseline criteria for conducting win/loss reviews. Not all opportunities require a win/loss review, nor is it desired. With proper design and clearly established criteria, win/loss reviews will become part of the normal daily opportunity management activities and rhythm, if not fully embedded within them.

When broadly and properly institutionalized, information and insights from win/loss reviews become a powerful reference tool for owners of active opportunities. When faced with a specific competitive scenario, the account teams can quickly access the tactical insights that helped other teams against a competitor. Even when not faced with an immediate need, sales teams will be attracted by the richness of information to browse through the reports to see how their peers are competing and winning, or what they learned from a loss. As each record tells a unique story, users often find themselves immersed in reading these micro-intelligence reports that chronicle a team's journey to victory or failure.

But to be able to reap the benefits from the past win/loss reviews, the reviews need to be captured first, and with a certain amount of quality and rigor that maximizes their value to others. Hence, there are two high-level process attributes that need monitoring: quantity and quality.

SCALE DRIVES QUANTITY

Beginning with process performance, it is important to define the baseline criteria for conducting win/loss reviews. For example, the entire opportunity set above a certain size, or against specific competitors, will form the denominator against which actual usage metrics are compared. This is commonly expressed as a percentage of win/loss reviews completed.

Regardless of how simple the process is, or how much it has been touted as a useful tool for helping sellers improve win rates, there will be the need to monitor process performance measure against preestablished criteria. These criteria need to be set by the business owners, not the information technology (IT) department. Overall process performance might be measured as a percentage of opportunities reviewed. This may give the process owners a target against which to monitor. For the win/loss review process described in this book, there needs to be a minimum quantity of new records on an ongoing basis to achieve statistical significance and a continuous knowledge flow from the shared insights.

For example, let's say your target calls for conducting a win/loss review for at least 50% of the opportunities won or lost whose value was greater $10,000. There were 100 opportunities that met these criteria last month, and there were 37 win/loss reviews conducted. Thirty-seven out of the 100 opportunities means that 37% completion was attained against a target of 50%, or a deficiency of -13%. Perhaps your target was set at 100% regardless of the opportunity size, but only when a specific competitor was involved. Additionally, you may call for different criteria depending on the outcome, for example, conducting a review for 75% of all wins, and 50% for all losses meeting a certain revenue amount. Additional guidance may be that there should be no more than a 3:1 ratio of reviews completed for wins and losses. This will ensure that there is a balance of learning. Otherwise, there may be some teams that review a disproportionately high number of wins, while ignoring the losses. Other teams may dismiss the value of the wins and review only losses, incorrectly assuming that there is learning only in losing. If your company allows "disengage" outcomes, it will be important to include these in the process and adjust the proportion accordingly.

There is no shortage of criteria that can be used during the baseline targets. But it should be noted that establishing a baseline for measuring process performance should not be confused with the actual policies set by various stakeholder groups who may have their own targets. Baseline targets can be useful in measuring expected process performance across an entire organization, and are useful for comparing the performance of different business units.

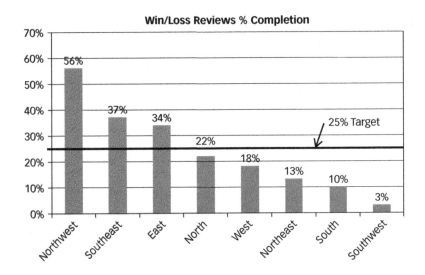

FIGURE 7.1 Percentage Completion of Win/Loss Reviews by Geographical Business Unit

Figure 7.1 shows how the process performance of different regions in a given geographical area may be compared. It shows not only performance against a common target, but also performance relative to other regions. This side-by-side comparison often appeals to the competitive nature of regional managers who strive to be among the highest performers in any given metric. Additional filters can be applied to show, for example, the percentage completion against specific competitors or product lines.

The targets set for conducting win/loss reviews depend on the needs of the business and the nuances of the industry, but it is important that the criteria be wide enough to ensure enough reviews will be completed to allow for data-driven analysis for several stakeholders. If the target completion bar is set too high, to the opportunity owner it may feel like an administrative burden and encourage a "checkbox exercise" mentality when conducting the reviews, which may reduce the quality of the input. Striking a balance between quantity and quality will require some trial and error to obtain the right baseline target. One should not be afraid to experiment, perhaps even choosing different targets within different regions to gauge and compare the performance.

QUALITY DRIVES VALUE

The other key attribute to monitor is the quality of the reviews being completed. Consider other processes where information quality is dependent on an individual's input and where the resulting quality is a challenge for your sales organizations. Account plans, proposals, presentations, customer relationship management (CRM) records, and forecasts typically have wide variability in quality. Left unchecked, the quality of these activities will likely deteriorate, which will significantly diminish their value to the sales process. Seller-driven win/loss reviews can suffer the same ailments as any other human-driven process, but as discussed in Chapter 1, the peer-review nature of this process has a sort of built-in mechanism for promoting higher quality. When properly executed with the full energy and discipline characteristic of a high-performing sales team, the quality and resulting value to the organization are greatly increased.

So how is quality of individual win/loss reviews measured? Another benefit of the institutionalized process is that the information that is captured will be reused in other areas of the business. For example, in the monthly sales review and forecast meetings, a sales manager may utilize only the information from the win/loss review reports to conduct a business review of deals won, lost, or disengaged over the prior month. Product managers will also rely on the reporting function to read the seller verbatims relevant to their product line. Competitive intelligence may also read the narratives and perform additional analytics to observe competitive trends when different analytical filters are applied. If a seller knows that his information is actually being read and contributes to creating a better product or service, this will often be incentive enough to ensure that the information being requested is thoughtful, is of high quality, and can be clearly understood by anyone who reviews it.

Even so, there is a need to monitor quality on an ongoing basis. Spot-checking and visual analysis are two commonly used quality inspection mechanisms. For example, win/loss review process owners may periodically look at a random sampling of reviews. In those samples they may inspect for missing or incorrect data that suggest some technological issues. They will look to see that the factors for the outcome were selected. And in the brief verbatims, they will look for a narrative that can be understood on its own, or at minimum, support the factors previously selected. Another simple mechanism is to view a report that shows several records per page. A quick visual inspection might reveal that a team is repeating the exact narratives for all of their reviews (e.g., copy/ paste), or that there are none at all. Patterns will quickly emerge from visual inspection that can then be called to the attention of the sales manager, for example.

It is important that quality guidance be a part of the training or reference materials designed for the win/loss review process. Accountability for assuring quality should rest with the sale managers.

VALUE, EXPECTATIONS, AND POLICY

For a win/loss review system to be an institutionalized and sustainable activity, there are three fundamental conditions that must be met: (1) value to the front-line sellers, (2) expectations that the information will be used in multiple scenarios, and (3) clear policy guidance that spells out the performance indicators. We arrived at the three high-level success factors from years of analysis and experimentation. While some specific factor names may be different, the general theme is the same: There must be a combination of incentives, standards, and rules.

As the quality and quantity of the win/loss review process outputs (business and competitive intelligence) are highly dependent on the informed inputs by the sales teams, the value proposition for sales must be clearly defined. The act of actually capturing the insights into a tool is not in itself a very exciting endeavor and the payoff is not immediate. Like other sales activities, even win/loss reviews can be regarded as administrative overhead if their value to the seller is not clear. This may lead to less rigorous reviews and energy placed in the process. Our aim is to avoid the checkbox mentality of just going through the motions with the uninspired goal of achieving a completion target.

For the input activity, one can quickly show how the process-enabled win/loss reviews actually save the sellers time and free them up to plan and sell. For example, if sellers have to document their postmortem in a lengthy word-processor template, spreadsheet, or presentation slide deck, it can easily be shown how the process might reduce their time burden by 80% or more. Since most of the information is pulled in from the CRM, and the factors are predefined and selected with a few clicks, and the narratives limited to just a few lines of text, it should take the sellers no more than 10 to 15 minutes to capture their insights and complete the review! That may seem absurd to those who think that it usually takes hours to do a postmortem on a complex deal. The reality is that most of the time spent doing postmortems on complex deals is spent on formatting and reentry of data that already exists elsewhere. And when the vice president sends out a request for a summary of key wins and losses for an ad hoc meeting with the chief executive officer (CEO), think of all the scrambling that takes place to reassemble the same information again, perhaps in a different format. The disruption to the sales leaders can be significant. This will resonate with many readers, because this scenario plays out time after time in the daily lives of sales teams. Knowing that minimal up-front work in capturing the information will save time, relieve stress, and provide accurate reports on demand is of great value.

For the value proposition that really speaks to "what's in it for me," a seller will soon realize that the information contributed by her peers around the world is information that speaks directly to her in her unique situation. Knowing that she is part of an information ecosystem that creates value as the insights get shared and leveraged is a powerful motivator. You will recall that in a previous survey sellers said they trust information from their peers over any other source, motivating the sellers to reciprocate with equally valuable insights.

Providing evidence of value is yet another way to ensure that the stakeholders, especially salespeople, see the value. Although sellers are trained to sell, or rather to guide their customers within the buying process, they themselves do not like to be "sold to." Over time you will have captured enough data to draw correlations between win rates and win/loss reviews. Your evidence will show that the teams that conduct win/loss reviews as a normal sales activity experience an average win rate that is 10% to 15% higher than those that do not. It is important to note that the correlation may not necessarily be causal, but perhaps one of many contributing factors that a well-tuned and disciplined sales team exhibits.

One more activity that provides a more direct view to a strong value proposition is integrating the win/loss review process with rewards and recognition processes. Although focused more on the win side of the equation, the process gains familiarity whether it is for wins or losses. We examine this concept in Chapter 6, "Beyond Competitive Insights."

SETTING EXPECTATIONS

One advantage of having an initiative become institutionalized is that it sets a base-level expectation that it is standard operating procedure (SOP). Consider some well-established processes within your organization that are being done without giving them much thought. When filing an expense report, for example, you are expected to use a particular process if you want your manager to approve the expense reimbursement. There really is no other way to be reimbursed, and so there is no resistance to the process.

For win/loss reviews, there are a number of ways to set the expectation that doing them is just SOP. A sales manager may set the expectation that closed opportunity reviews be conducted using only the reports that come directly from win/loss reviews. The manager pulls up the report to discuss those opportunities that were won or lost over the prior month. The seller begins to highlight a key win that occurred, but the manager asks why it is not in the report. The disciplined sales manager will remind the seller that since it is not in the reports, it will not be covered during the review. This reinforces the expectation that to discuss the opportunity during the sale review it must first be captured in the win/loss review process.

Product and marketing teams may also set expectations by establishing win/loss reviews as an important part of the feedback loop. Say, for example, that a sales team just lost a major deal and that customer feedback indicated that in this case it was truly a deficiency with product capability. The sales team sends an email directly to the group product manager with the feedback. Having already established the win/loss review as the primary source for opportunity-specific customer feedback, the product manager asks the seller to capture the feedback within the established process. The aim is to encourage the use of a process that may already have several dependent stakeholders. Again, this reinforces the expectation that the institutionalized win/loss review process is part of the SOP for transmitting customer feedback to the product teams.

Setting expectations for conducting win/loss reviews should be part of the onboarding and training process for those who are new to a role or new to the company. Typically they would be part of the overall sales training curriculum that includes account planning, relationship management, opportunity management, forecasting, and pipeline management.

POLICY CONSIDERATIONS

Policies governing the activity of performing win/loss reviews depend largely on the goals of the program itself. One policy might be an orientation for reviewing major or complex deals where the deal value sets the marker. For example, there may be a base-level policy that states that all opportunities won or lost over €100,000 require a completed win/loss review. Other policies may focus on a particular competitor or product line.

In the early stages of implementing a win/loss review program, it is a common mistake to set the bar too high. Requiring that 100% of all opportunities have a win/loss review is destined to disappoint the win/loss review program manager, but more importantly, the opportunity owners will feel that the administrative overhead is too taxing on their selling time. Experience has shown that for account teams that manage 20 to 30 active opportunities each year, 30% is actually a more reasonable target. And that number might be higher if we were to apply baseline criteria that reduced the total opportunities that would be targeted for a review. For example, out of 30 managed opportunities over the course of a year, if we were to apply the baseline criterion of €100,000 or greater, the total number that qualified for a review might actually be 15 of them. It is not unreasonable to set the baseline target to 50% or higher in this case.

Now that the policy targets are set, the attainment of these targets can be reported in a dashboard or some management reports. One method of attaining policy compliance is to simply show the rankings against attainment targets. Rankings can be organized by geographic region, by subregion, and even by individual seller. Measuring usage performance can provide win/loss review program managers with additional insights that may reveal root causes for underperforming utilization. A more detailed treatment of *root-cause analysis* is discussed in Appendix A, "Process Improvement: A Case Study."

MEASURING OUTCOME PERFORMANCE

A typical metric for measuring outcome performance is the overall win rate. There are two primary views of win rates: the percentages as a function of *counts* and of *revenue*. It is common to look only at the counts to determine win rates, or the impact that the factors that contributed to a particular outcome had on the outcome. This misses the more important determinant of performance: revenue. To illustrate this point, let us use ten deals won and lost whose aggregate value equaled €100. Out of those ten opportunities, seven of them were won; the other three were lost or deferred. It would be easy to conclude that your win rate was 70% (seven wins divided by ten total opportunities).

Now, let's assume that the total *value* of those seven wins equaled €25. The real win rate is now only 25%! The picture no longer looks quite so bright. One can also apply this logic to the *factors* attributed to wins and losses. For example, if a factor such as sales team performance was cited by your customers as contributing to only 10% of your losses, you might overlook that the value of those same deals accounted for over 50% of the revenue from the same set of opportunities. Failure to measure win-rate performance as a function of revenue (in addition to counts) will likely lead to faulty conclusions, poorly constructed strategies, and potentially disastrous results.

To obtain a clearer picture of win-rate performance, one must look beyond a point in time. Measuring win rates over time can reveal startling trends, especially when they are filtered against specific competitors, range of opportunity sizes, or product and service lines. The data here may reflect the actual opportunity outcomes logged in the CRM, not what is captured by the win/loss reviews. Viewing only what is captured in the win/loss review database may show that some teams or regions disproportionately favor reviews of losses over wins, or vice versa.

A common way of measuring win rates over time is to observe them by the total *number* of opportunities. In this method the numerator is the win count, and the denominator is the total count of opportunities. As suggested in Figure 7.2, the win rates for this company over the past 12 months suggest a steady increase in win rates when measured as a function of the number of opportunities. The data also suggests a corresponding trend reduction in losses. For the most part, the disengaged opportunities trend remained fairly flat over this period, which also suggests that the dynamic is between the wins and losses.

Comparing these trends with the information garnered through the win/loss review process, one can begin to connect the dots and uncover additional insights into this performance trend.

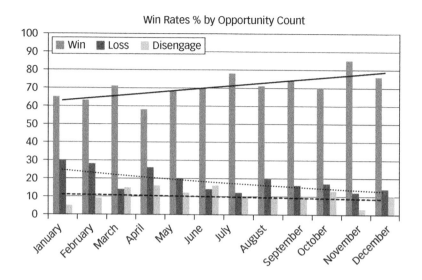

FIGURE 7.2   Win Rates Percentage as a Function of Count

In the hypothetical scenario shown in Figure 7.2, clearly the company is experiencing a significant increase in win rates from about 63% at the beginning of the year to nearly 79% toward the end of the year. The 16% improvement in win rates is something most companies should celebrate. However, increasing win rates do not necessarily translate into increasing revenues and earnings.

In Figure 7.3, we see the same hypothetical company using the same performance data, but this time viewing the win rates as a percentage of revenue.

Immediately, we notice a dramatic downtrend in win rates in just the same 12-month period. This suggests that even though the wins as a function of the total number of opportunities are increasing, the average value of each opportunity may be decreasing. This means that the company is winning more but earning less. This could also have a major effect on profit margins as the average cost of each sale is increasing.

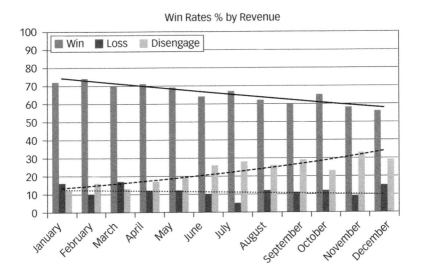

FIGURE 7.3   Win Rates Percentage as a Function of Revenue

   Although the loss rates are relatively steady, the significant rise in the disengaged opportunities may mask problems that otherwise would not be detected. For example, further investigation might reveal that the complexity of opportunities is increasing to the point where the sales teams are beyond their capability to compete and are therefore shifting their focus to the smaller, lower-hanging fruit. Sales teams may be inclined to walk away earlier rather than spend any more energy on an opportunity they feel will end up as a loss. This could indicate misalignment between what the product teams are producing and the ability of the sales teams to effectively compete. Perhaps the resourcing model is heavily weighted on a particular product set that is nearing the end of its lifecycle. There could be many reasons for this trend behavior.

SUMMARY

- An effective win/loss review process includes the capability for measuring not only the win rates against specific competitors, but also the performance of the process itself.
- Win/loss reviews need to capture data with a certain level of quality and rigor so as to maximize their value to others.
- Monitoring process health includes measuring utilization scale and quality.
- Minimum-quantity targets are necessary to drive statistically relevant insights.
- The quality of reviews can be randomly checked by looking at specific opportunities as well as trends viewed in aggregate. The narratives will give good insights as to the rigor applied.
- For a win/loss review system to be an institutionalized and sustainable activity, there are three fundamental conditions that must be met: (1) value, (2) expectations, and (3) clear policy guidance.
- Opportunity outcome performance is measured as a function of both opportunity count and opportunity revenue. Together, these measures will reveal unique insights for sales performance.

CHAPTER 8

STAKEHOLDER AND CULTURAL CONSIDERATIONS

Knowledge is multiplied by the simple process of sharing it when it may serve others.

—Business proverb

Few business processes can claim the wide swath of stakeholders who are either directly affected or have a stake in the outcomes of the win/loss review process. For some, the information and insights are directly actionable; for others, the intelligence gained is used to inform sales and marketing strategy; for still others, it serves as a critical product or service feedback loop.

For a win/loss review program to have any chance of successfully realizing its true value (and its intended purpose), it must have input and buy-in from a number of stakeholder groups. While the focus for the program design remains primarily on the value to the front-line sellers of the capture and use of the insights gained, several stakeholder groups will have their business requirements

Professions and Roles	Benefits of Win/Loss Reviews											
	Structured Deal Reviews	Reference Knowledge Base	Account Plan Facilitation	Coaching and Training	Org. Design and Resourcing	Brand Image and Awareness	Value Proposition Development	Sales Collateral and Tools	Competitive Displacement	Product Road Map	Cost Efficacy	Risk Management
Account Manager	•	•	•			•		•	•	•		
Sales Specialist		•	•			•			•			
Sales Manager	•			•		•		•	•		•	
Sales Director	•			•	•			•	•	•		•
VP Sales				•	•		•	•	•			•
Services Manager	•	•	•			•			•		•	•
Territory/Regional Leader	•	•				•		•	•			•
Product Manager				•			•	•	•	•		
Marketing Manager				•		•	•		•			
Competitive Intelligence Manager		•		•					•			•
Finance									•		•	•
Corporate Leadership					•	•	•		•	•	•	•

FIGURE 8.1 Stakeholder Benefits Matrix

reflected in what the win/loss program actually delivers (e.g., reports, analytics, and management capabilities).

By including multidisciplinary stakeholder groups from the outset, benefits are realized much sooner and little time is wasted in rearchitecting the process to accommodate business requirements otherwise missed in the early stages of development. Further, as many will have invested time and energy in the planning and development, they will usually feel a sense of ownership and accountability for its continued success.

The matrix in Figure 8.1 gives a glimpse of the areas benefiting from the win/loss review process. This is not intended to be an exhaustive list, but rather to suggest the broad set of stakeholders who can directly benefit from the insights gained.

ACCOUNT MANAGER

The account manager is the primary stakeholder of the win/loss review process. When considering the design, flow, sales process integration, and outputs, the seller's voice must be considered first when architecting the sales-originated win/loss review process.

As the content originators and the primary consumers of actionable insights, members of the account team have the most skin in the game and stand to benefit most from this process. There's a minimal up-front time investment required to capture outcomes that may or may not have an immediate perceived payback. Whereas information captured can be immediately used by other salespeople and account teams, it is when enough volume has been collected that relevant and strategic insights begin to crystallize.

The process of capturing the information from a win or a loss is the time to reflect on the dynamics of the deal. A typical salesperson will be asked at some point to review with his manager the outcomes of opportunities that have been won or lost. There are often many formats for gathering and reporting this information during sales meetings. Among these are offline spreadsheets or the ubiquitous PowerPoint presentation. There is a significant amount of energy and time spent preparing these documents, if they are prepared at all, and the emphasis is often on the formatting, not the substance. Preparation for sales meetings usually accounts for most of the pain felt by a salesperson on a day-to-day basis. Many readers will immediately identify with this pain. Whether completed through a customer relationship management (CRM) system or an integrated CRM module that allows for capture at the point where the opportunity status is changed, an integrated win/loss review process greatly improves efficiencies and virtually eliminates the redundancies and overhead associated with reporting deal outcomes.

Where sellers most benefit from this process is in having access to the knowledge base of insights composed of other seller entries, and applying those actionable insights to their active opportunities. This is facilitated by a simple search query that allows sellers to select specific criteria about past deals that most closely match their current situation. The richness of shared information and the ability to produce personalized reports are characteristics of a "mesh" business.[1]

Here we emphasize that this is a seller-to-seller loop that shares and consumes valuable front-line intelligence that might be unpolished but is highly relevant. Just as we earlier emphasized that we must begin to trust the sellers with providing us with valuable insights, sellers typically will trust the information generated by their peers over that which is highly polished or publicly available.

For the account manager:

- Value is realized if the process helps exceed quota, improves chances for getting recognized, improves competitiveness, saves time from administrative tasks, and provides access to successful sales practices by peers.

- Deliverables for this audience are a simple application interface for capture and reporting, preferably integrated with CRM, and informative training and guidance material.
- Potential resistance may be encountered due to the imposition on selling time and exposure of personal skill deficiencies; it might be viewed as an inspection mechanism.

SALES MANAGER

Sales managers have numerous accountabilities for managing sales and leading their teams. At a high level, they are charged with recruiting, developing, and managing the performance of sales individuals, managing their business according to established sales processes, and working in close collaboration with extended teams and sales leadership to drive sales results. For sales processes, they conduct sales pipeline reviews, submit sales forecasts, review account plans, and with increasing frequency, review opportunity outcomes.

With the mounting pressures of today's business climate, sales managers are often focused on the transactional nature of sales and reporting, or "the numbers." The reason why post-opportunity outcome reviews are not as vigorously executed is that the information is more qualitative and requires *transformational* (versus transactional) thinking to reveal new opportunities for growth and to turn the insights into meaningful action.

Properly implemented, the win/loss review process will quickly be embraced as a value-add process and coaching opportunity for account teams.

For the sales manager:

- Value is realized if the process accelerates pipeline velocity, improves forecast accuracy, facilitates sales coaching and recognition of teams, enhances team discipline, improves customer retention, differentiates seller performance, and reduces administrative overhead.

- Deliverables for this audience are standard and custom management reports, exportable reports for custom analysis, and capability for recognizing key wins.
- Potential resistance may be encountered due to a lack of skills to coach or analyze the outcomes, an added process on top of a growing number of accountabilities, and perception of intrusion on customer face-time.

PRODUCT MANAGER

The role of product manager in any company is usually one of the most complex as it intersects with many functional areas— sales, marketing, product development, services, support, and so on. Ironically, it is also a role that most often requires the ability to influence without authority. Building alliances and influence requires a combination of skills and business acumen. By being integral players in the win/loss review process, product managers will have access to timely customer feedback through the sales process and a platform on which to build and strengthen cross-functional collaboration. More detailed reviews can be facilitated with the help of the sales teams and in select cases can be followed up on directly with the customer.

Information from win/loss reviews can also help inform and prioritize the feature deliverables in a product road map. Assumptions can be validated with hard data as well as with anecdotal evidence. Product managers will have more insights into the sales dynamics, which can help them formulate training and readiness materials for their sales teams. A new competitor making inroads into accounts will often catch product teams unprepared to assist sales with product positioning and training materials.

Product managers will also benefit from a continuous flow of feedback around key product features, especially features that are missing or flawed. Aggregating these insights can help determine the scope of the issues as to whether they are one-off or broad scale.

A product manager who notices a disturbing trend with a product, perhaps one that is found in the majority of losses, can confidently assemble a group of account managers and lay out the findings that come from the aggregated feedback. Sales teams will appreciate the fact that their feedback is being heard and acted upon. The clarity of the feedback will reduce or remove any ambiguity as to what is being asked for, allow for feature/fix prioritization for upcoming releases, and make the dialogue with product development teams more fruitful and relevant.

However, a challenge that many product managers face is obtaining enough data to be statistically relevant. As earlier discussed, having enough data allows for meaningful analysis of the factors affecting the sales outcome. And since many of the factors are indeed product related, with enough data it is a relatively simple matter to determine whether product features had some bearing on the outcomes. With strong empirical evidence, the product manager can confidently recommend data-driven product enhancements, or perhaps retire a product altogether.

A well-crafted and integrated win/loss review process will provide several bridges into other areas of your company as it is already designed with broad stakeholder requirements.

For the product manager:

- Value is realized if there is immediate access to postmortems where the manager can probe for product-related issues and feedback; feedback is timely and actionable; insights are useful for enhancing existing products and providing ideas for new products.

- Deliverables for this audience are standard and custom management reports by product and analysis capabilities by product features. Additional guidance can be provided on contacting sales teams for individual or group debriefs.
- Potential resistance may be due to field teams not capturing enough information, or not trusting that the data being captured by sales is accurate and unbiased.

MARKETING MANAGER

Marketing managers are responsible for influencing the level, timing, and composition of customer demand. Rapidly emerging forces of globalization have compelled firms to market beyond the borders of their home country, making international marketing highly significant and an integral part of a firm's marketing strategy. This same dynamic has introduced increased competitive risks that must be factored. Relying on traditional domestic market and competitive intelligence sources may not reveal the nuances of emerging competitive threats in another country. The win/loss review process that incorporates field insights from the sales offices within a country will often fill that gap if there are no local marketing teams who might otherwise provide the local intelligence from primary and secondary sources.

Competitor analysis is an essential component of corporate marketing strategy, yet most firms do not systematically conduct this type of competitive deal analysis. Instead, many enterprises operate on what Fleisher and Bensoussan called "informal impressions, conjectures, and intuition gained through the tidbits of information about competitors every manager continually receives."[2] As a result, traditional environmental scanning places many firms at risk of dangerous competitive blind spots due to a lack of robust competitor analysis.

Legal and trade rules add to the complexity of the marketing manager's duties. A win/loss review program can provide a window into the field practices that border on breaking or bending established rules. For example, a marketing manager who notices an extraordinary increase in wins due to pricing practices may inquire to see if teams are ignoring or going around pricing policies, which could be considered predatory. A large number of losses due to local regulations may inform the marketing teams that they are in breach of warranties or safety regulations.

For the marketing manager:

- Value is realized if primary and secondary market research is augmented or validated; feedback from field teams reveals changes in brand value and perception; new approaches are suggested for new customer acquisition.
- Deliverables for this audience are standard and custom management reports by customer type and geography that provide insights into price, product, and promotion strategies.
- Potential resistance may be encountered due to field teams not capturing enough information, or data that is considered too high level.

CORPORATE LEADERSHIP

Defining and leading the corporate vision and mission, growing shareholder value, developing strategic direction, and monitoring and assessing risks are among the accountabilities of corporate officers. Corporate officers are charged with managing the present-day business, but knowing which business strategies to discard and which strategies to pursue for future growth is just as important. However, understanding the reasons why sales deals are won or lost is one of the biggest blind spots for corporate leaders.

The sales teams that have direct and sustained customer interactions are the ones that deliver the last mile of customer value and stand closest to the "moments of truth." Yet, information from customer engagements that trickles up and across the organization through traditional reporting and review loops is highly anecdotal and has likely been filtered and adjusted to suit the needs of the messenger.

Whether in a publicly traded company or a private one, understanding the effects of competitive forces on a company's business forecasts can significantly influence guidance to shareholders. By reviewing the competitive trends over time and uncovering the influencing factors, financial officers and analysts can more accurately assess how significant a threat may be, and feel more confident in their overall business assessment and outlook. Shareholders will like to know that even if there are certain unfavorable competitive trends, corporate leaders understand them and are taking action to mitigate their risks. At the same time, the shareholders seek evidence that there are signs of robust business health and long-term growth.

AN EMERGING CAREER SKILL AND ROLE REQUIREMENT

As the previous stakeholder summaries emphasize, win/loss reviews affect a wide stakeholder audience, and any implementation of such a discipline should take into account the needs of the stakeholders. Indeed, a stakeholder analysis is one of the most critical exercises to conduct if the program is to have any chance of long-term success.

The online job postings in Figure 8.2 suggest that win/loss review skills are becoming increasingly sought after in a variety of careers in both sales and marketing, and at all levels. The term *win/loss* is fairly loosely defined and it is assumed that the reader knows what it means.

Sales Roles

Account Manager—"Contribute timely and quality information on industry, market, competition, account status, and *win-loss analysis.*"

Channel Sales—"Responsible for completing and communicating *win/loss reports* to appropriate management staff."

Global Sales Director —"Providing feedback regarding market trends, pricing, *win/loss data*, and competition to product management, commercial operations, and Smart Grid P&L, ensuring new product/solution offerings meet customer/market needs and timing."

Inside Sales Manager—"Builds, monitors, and orchestrates sales pipelines to ensure continuous population of near- and long-term opportunities; manages the size, shape, and quality of pipeline; analyzes overall win rates and *win/loss ratios.*"

Practice Sales—"Analyze trends, cycle timelines, and *win/loss* ratios."

Sales Specialist—"Develop and execute tactical and strategic sales plans; create and manage sales funnel and forecast; establish and drive evaluation unit investment plan; capture and share **win/loss competitive experiences.**"

Senior Business Development Manager—"Responsible for development and effective management of personnel, comp plans, sales pipeline, forecasting, *win-loss reporting*, CRM tools, marketing programs, and account management policies that support company revenue and profit goals and objectives, and attaining an established quota."

Senior Program Manager—"Define and provide project management of account review, big deal review, and *win/loss review.*"

VP Sales Operations—"Manage all sales employee feedback via surveys (i.e., *win/loss* and employee satisfaction)."

Marketing Roles

Pricing Analyst—"Responsibilities include: pricing strategy, business/market segment models; leading indicator reports; competitive analysis. Manage/influence key marketing/sales business processes (MRD, quote, pricing, *win/loss*, competitive insight, product lifecycle management."

Product Manager—"Establish formal and informal channels of communication with customers and partners to collect insight on needs, usage scenarios, *win/loss analysis*, and success stories."

Product Marketing Manager—"Directs research of product lines to pricing maintenance, competitive analysis, *win/loss analysis*, historical sales analysis, and monitoring of all industry innovations."

Product Marketing Director—"Sales collaboration: Identify, prioritize sales tools and marketing materials required by sales and perform and manage **win/loss analysis** process. Produce head-to-head competition reports and perform and manage *win/loss analysis* process."

VP Product Marketing—"Gather and analyze service/product performance, operational metrics, and *win/loss analysis.*"

FIGURE 8.2 Jobs Requiring Win/Loss Review Skills

Those who are responsible for designing sales role strategies in their companies often overlook win/loss reviews as a core activity. In companies with less formal structures for managing roles, the task of recruiting and developing is left up to the hiring manager. It is important that expectations for conducting win/loss reviews be set up front by updating job descriptions, hiring guides, and even performance plans. Below are some examples of simple statements that can be easily embedded in these documents:

- **Job description:** "Conducts and logs unbiased opportunity reviews and analysis, utilizing the corporate win/loss review system on a timely basis."
- **Hiring guide:** "Candidate demonstrates evidence of being accountable and self-critical, and will reflect these competencies in the conduct of unbiased win/loss reviews."
- **Performance plan:** "To conduct unbiased win/loss reviews on at least 50% of opportunities won or lost that meet established criteria."

CORPORATE AND LEADERSHIP CULTURE

The role that business and social cultures play in understanding and acting on the forces that impact your business cannot be overstated. In a learning-oriented organization, the culture allows self-criticism, encourages constructive feedback toward others, and promotes a high level of transparency. The resulting dynamic is that "one competes from a common playbook, makes data-driven decisions, and promotes cross-group collaboration, alignment and execution."[3]

Corporate cultures can vary greatly among companies, and even within the same company. Here, *corporate* doesn't necessarily mean the corporate headquarters. There often exist varying interpretations of the explicitly stated corporate culture across geographies, business groups, and teams. So why, then, are cultures not so uniformly distributed and adopted?

Cultural norms found among nations and ethnic groups also play a significant role in the shaping of business culture. In a particular country, "saving face" might override any corporate value statements around learning and sharing, as well as directives to document and analyze losses on a regular basis and in a meaningful way. At the same time, a culture of humility and reserve may hide very compelling insights for wins.

As it relates to win/loss reviews, culture is strongly influenced by the disposition that senior leaders have and the messages they send to their organizations. Do they have a win-at-all-costs mentality with a low tolerance for losing? Do the core messages change and depend on whether you are "making your numbers"? And if you're in a winning trend, does the discourse still focus on continuous improvement?

For sellers, the results of a sales engagement are black and white — either they've won or lost the deal. When a seller wins, there are the usual accolades that get sent out in broad emails, recognizing key contributors, and the subsequent torrent of congratulatory reply messages from senior management and executives. Many times the sales teams driving these wins go on to receive special awards or other sales incentives, and deservedly so. If one were to look closely at one of these recognition emails, one would find a rich set of factors that contributed to that win. Typically, we see a top-level deal summary, the amount of revenue generated, the products and solutions involved, the partner strategy, and of course, the people who made it all possible.

The amount of energy that goes into crafting the carefully worded email is often immense. The sad truth about this is that the insights are usually short-lived and go unrecycled. Rarely does this information get captured in a way that forms a knowledge base for active deals in the pipeline. Would it be too much to ask to utilize a process that offers the same level of recognition but captures the information in a usable way? Now, what if we were to tie in the win/loss review process to the same recognition or sales incentive programs already established in your company? For wins, reviews can form the base layer of information that can feed into a number of sales incentive programs, contests, or the ubiquitous "winwires." To achieve greater acceptance, the win/loss review process can be the prerequisite step that captures the factors and the accompanying narratives. This information can then feed into any number of connected business processes and be adjusted or parsed in a way that suits the particular need of each process. The synergies gained by aligning the processes are immense.

Obviously, there are no incentives for losing. But there can be incentives for thoughtfully documenting and sharing the key lessons that come from losses. A growing practice, but one still much less frequent than announcing a win, is announcing a loss. Whereas this was unheard of as recently as five years ago, an informal survey revealed that about 25% of companies are seeing an increase in documented losses in similar fashion that a win is announced. Typically, however, losses are discussed behind closed doors within the domain of business reviews and forecast updates. They may be reviewed along with a long list of deals that were won or lost. While the more important lost deals will get their share of attention and scrutiny, prevailing business culture will often suppress the documentation of the causes of the loss or fail to make it usable to a broader audience. Again, the energy spent on documentation is short-lived and it is not recycled into a reusable knowledge base.

CULTURE AND SOCIAL NETWORKS

Another well-known force that is shaping business culture is the proliferation of social networking and penetration of social software. It is often referred to as the "consumerization of IT," and businesses can no longer afford to ignore its influence on corporate culture. Information technology (IT) departments have been forced to recognize the phenomenon, primarily from a security perspective. Many employees install and use instant messaging clients or other peer networking programs, often breaching corporate IT security protocols. Training and readiness teams recognized early that content and product rating systems similar to those found on online retailers such as Amazon are providing valuable insights to improve their internal and external offerings. Marketing and product teams are using direct feedback loops from employees and customers to get real-time feedback from early adopters

> The "coolness" of using social-networking-like interfaces is actually encouraging sellers to participate without the need for stringent policy enforcement.

and broader audiences. Executives, too, are jumping on board with internal blog posts that are replacing the static monthly or quarterly newsletter with more interactive media formats.

In a recently published whitepaper, Erin Traudt and Rich Vancil of IDC state:

> IDC views social software as an enabler to the cultural shift and business process changes that need to take place in order to transform a company into a social business. This journey toward becoming a social business is not without challenges and takes time, effort, and commitment. However, the positive outcomes can translate into a more open, efficient, and innovative organization that has deeper employee and customer relationships, quicker decision-making capabilities, and speed-to-market potential.[4]

The point here is to highlight the sociocultural shift permeating corporate cultures toward sharing personal insights and opinions with the expectation that it is contributing to a greater good for everyone, not only oneself. This "indirect reciprocity" represents a shift from an earlier time when doing something good for someone came with the expectation that the favor would be directly returned. Now, the return is expected to come not merely from a single person or a small group, but from thousands of people who have benefited in some way from the contributor's generosity.[5]

As it applies to win/loss reviews, this cultural shift is creating new and fascinating opportunities to capture and share insights from peers. Not only does technology make it simple to conduct self-guided reviews, but the "coolness" of using social-networking-like interfaces is actually encouraging sellers to participate without the need for stringent policy enforcement.

So the discussion around losses needs to take on a tone of learning and course corrections, not of assigning blame or threats of job loss. This speaks again to the core values a company's leadership espouses. Only by encouraging and practicing a culture of learning and being self-critical can we create the cultural environment that permits this open and disarmingly honest dialogue.

SOCIAL MEDIA PARADIGMS

The younger generation now entering sales careers have been part of the social media phenomenon since their childhood and are more comfortable with the paradigms of consuming and sharing information with the masses, not only within their personal relationships. They have developed ways of replacing lengthy conversations with short bursts of information without compromising the intended message. Even Baby Boomers, Gen-Xers, and those who are even remotely associated with information technology and social networking are adjusting to the evolving language of social media.

What this paradigm is doing to the integrity of the written (and spoken) language and its governing structure is to be debated elsewhere.

Consider the two example narratives describing customer concerns and how they were addressed, captured as part of the same post-opportunity outcome review. Both narratives offer the same insights that may be useful to someone in a similar situation.

Example 2, while significantly shorter than the first, provides the same useful insights and actually complies with the 140-character limit of a tweet on Twitter! This paradigm, often found in one-to-many social networks, is creating the ideal scenario for capturing the insights from sales transactions in a concise and mixed–structure format.[6]

EXAMPLE 1

"The customer expressed concern over the scalability of the solution and whether they were going to have to rip and replace their existing infrastructure, since they've invested over $2 million over the past three years. There was also a lot invested in the skills to operate their current system and any major overhaul would severely disrupt their business operations. We were able to address their concerns by showing that we could leverage most of their existing platforms and provide the scalability needed to address growth. The new skills needed were minimal and the training workshop was negotiated into the final contract at no extra charge."

EXAMPLE 2

"Cust raised scale, legacy investments/exist'g skills, effect on ops. Solution leveraged core infra and skills, added training @close"

SUMMARY

- The win/loss review process has a broad stakeholder audience who either are directly affected by or have a stake in the outcomes of the win/loss review process.
- Successful implementation and value realization rely on input and buy-in from a number of multidisciplinary stakeholder groups.
- The account manager is the primary stakeholder of the win/loss review process. When evaluating the design, flow, sales process integration, and outputs, the seller's voice must be considered first in architecting the sales-originated win/loss review process.
- Although information captured can be immediately used by other salespeople and account teams, it is when enough volume has been collected that relevant and strategic insights begin to crystallize.
- Those responsible for designing sales role strategies in their companies often overlook win/loss reviews as a core activity. It is important that expectations for conducting win/loss reviews be set up front by updating job descriptions, hiring guides, and performance plans.
- Several other stakeholders such as sales managers, product and marketing managers, and corporate leadership have an interest in the win/loss review process.
- Skills to conduct or manage win/loss review programs are becoming increasingly sought after in a variety of careers in both sales and marketing, and at all levels.
- Business and social cultures are important forces that must be considered when implementing a win/loss review program. Corporate cultures can vary greatly across companies, and even within the same company.
- Cultural norms found among nations and ethnic groups also play a significant role in the shaping of business culture.

- A win/loss review system can leverage the energies used in providing seller recognition and rewards by harnessing the insights being captured as part of those processes. There can also be incentives for thoughtfully documenting losses.
- Social networks are impacting corporate cultures by providing more fluid communications among employees and the corporate leadership.

NOTES

1. L. Gansky, *The Mesh: Why the Future of Business Is Sharing* (New York: Penguin Group, 2010). Four characteristics are described in a mesh business, and the process discussed here reflects all but the "physical goods." The other characteristics include community sharing, advanced digital networks, and elements of social networks. It can be argued that intellectual goods are part of the mesh business as the author cites several examples of intellectual property that is rented for a period of time. For example, Netflix rents movies. The physical medium is just used to transport the intellectual property.
2. C. S. Fleisher and B. E. Bensoussan, *Business and Competitive Analysis: Effective Application of New and Classic Methods* (Upper Saddle River, NJ: FT Press, 2007).
3. B. Aziza and J. Fitts, *Drive Business Performance: Enabling a Culture of Intelligent Execution* (New York: John Wiley & Sons, 2008), p. 19. Aziza and Fitts explore the broader dimensions of corporate culture in the context of business intelligence capabilities.
4. E. Traudt and R. Vancil, "IDC White Paper: Becoming a Social Business: The IBM Story," Framingham, MA: International Data Corporation, January 2011.
5. R. Botsman and R. Rogers, *What's Mine Is Yours: The Rise of Collaborative Consumption* (New York: HarperCollins, 2010). This book explores the rise of new economic models based on sharing, but reveals strong cultural shifts in the mindset of sharing information, and not only goods.
6. E. Qualman, *Socialnomics: How Social Media Transforms the Way We Live and Do Business* (Hoboken, NJ: John Wiley & Sons, 2009). The bridge between social media and seller-generated win/loss reviews is crystallized here in the way sellers create and consume content in short bursts.

CHAPTER 9

IMPLEMENTING A WIN/LOSS REVIEW PROGRAM

Clever talk can confound the workings of virtue, just as small impatiences can confound great projects.

—Confucius

Implementing a win/loss review process is similar to implementing most other business processes that aim to deliver specific outputs to internal or external customers. The origins of the win/loss review are similar to many other initiatives in that it is initiated to support a strategic business objective. And since we aim to deliver insights to a broad group of stakeholders, we are addressing the needs of several customers (see Chapter 8, "Stakeholder and Cultural Considerations").

To achieve the business goals of win/loss reviews, we adhere to the discipline of *business process management* (BPM). Through BPM, we combine process-centric and cross-functional approaches for an organization wishing to implement a win/loss review process.

As an information technology (IT)-enabled discipline, BPM promotes organizational agility and supports efforts of managers to drive process change and rapid innovation to better meet internal customer requirements and expectations.

Benchmarks are established using service-level agreements (SLAs) and key performance indicators (KPIs). Information derived from performance metrics is critical to driving the iterative process of optimizing the business practices that support organizational goals. That information is used to continually optimize business rules in real time—a process that enables rule change, versioning, and simple execution.

The process owner for win/loss reviews is often a program director, business analyst, or process architect, and generally comes from the business side of the organization. These individuals will have a strong understanding of IT, which is critical to effective interactions with the IT department. Process owners work across the organization because BPM is essentially cross-functional, involving the process owners, who are responsible for getting the day-to-day operational work done; department heads, who are responsible for managing divisional areas; and organizational leadership, providing oversight and direction.

ESTABLISHING BUSINESS GOALS AND OBJECTIVES

The first action to be taken by the core win/loss review program team is to create the *program goals and objectives*. The goals and objectives will be used to guide the requirements gathering activities, evaluate the requirements that are generated, and measure the overall success of the resulting implementation.

A win/loss review program can support a wide variety of goals. Goals are typically stated as broad-spectrum indications of a program's intentions. Some example goal statements include:

- "Operationalize the capture and use of field-generated competitive intelligence to a broad group of stakeholders."
- "Minimize the time between customer feedback and improvements in product feature road maps."
- "Enable strategic alignment between sales and marketing by standardizing on sources of customer feedback."

However, objectives contribute to the fulfillment of specified goals and are a way of evaluating the goals for an individual project. A common criterion for setting objectives is to use the *SMART* (*s*pecific, *m*easurable, *a*ttainable, *r*elevant, *t*ime-bound) acronym, a simple mnemonic used during the project's objective-setting stage. Examples of win/loss review objectives include:

- "Increase win-rate averages by 5% each quarter."
- "Reduce product returns by 10% by year-end."
- "Perform a win/loss review on 20% of deals within two weeks of a win or loss."

PLANNING PHASE

In complex organizations with sophisticated sales processes and tools, having a formal project plan is critical to the success of company-wide deployment of the win/loss review process. Most major organizations have dedicated resources, guidelines, or policies for project management and process improvement projects that facilitate planning and deployment of enterprise-wide initiatives. Less sophisticated applications or organizations may need comprehensive process and deployment plans. Regardless of the organization's size and complexity, a *plan* is necessary.

Although this chapter is focused on the larger and more complex business environment, the principles discussed can be applied across any business regardless of complexity.

The plan for a win/loss review program encompasses several activities and milestones. These include the identification of stakeholders, the elicitation of requirements, development and deployment of the program itself, and planned subsequent releases of the program. The plan should also include activities such as the communication program, post-implementation support, and business and political alignment efforts.

The plan will also evolve over time. As the program is executed, activities will surface that were not previously considered, approaches will evolve, and resourcing may change. As requirements are elicited they can and will change perspectives of what is needed and what is possible. All of these impact the plan so that it becomes a living document.

Based on your initial assessment of the program, you will identify an approach, outline the major activities and deliverables, and review this with the business and IT stakeholders. As you move forward through the program activities you will continue to update activities and time estimates and share the updates with your program team.

ELICITATION, DOCUMENTATION, AND REVIEW PHASE

Arguably the single most important activity in the process of implementing a win/loss review program, the collection and publication of the business requirements to be satisfied by the program is critical to all future activities.[1] This activity brings together the needs of all potential users of the system, documents them in a format that allows for clear understanding, comparison, priority setting, and pricing, and then allows for the creation of a formal release plan of a system/process to meet the requirements. These requirements are usually brought together and shared as part of a *business requirements document* (BRD). A *business requirement* is the assertion of business need that enables us to demonstrate greater business value with our internal customers and improve our effectiveness and efficiency.

Properly done, the process of developing the BRD gives the business owners insight as to what the organization really needs from the win/loss review system. It also provides supporting stakeholders (e.g., IT, engineering, human resources, etc.) an opportunity to collaborate and contribute up front, and an early view of what is required. If it is anticipated that the IT department will be an integral part of the solution delivery, they should be moved up the value chain and involved early in what they will be developing. This results in a more fruitful dialogue and a better outcome in terms of quality and effectiveness of the systems that are ultimately delivered.

While there are many methods of collecting business requirements, the following have been found to be particularly effective for a win/loss review program.

Interviewing

Personal interviews with a cross-section of stakeholders afford the interviewers the chance to ask a set of prepared questions but also allow them to explore answers so they can gain additional insight. To conduct an interviewing campaign, you need to first create a questionnaire. If you are also going to conduct a survey to distribute broadly to stakeholder organizations, your interview questionnaire should closely match the survey. To obtain the most value from the interview effort, you should send the questionnaire out in advance of the interview and include the business objectives as context. Conduct the interview and capture initial answers to the questions posed and then the results of the more detailed discussion.

Close the interview by verbally summarizing results and requesting permission to contact the subject again to clarify or explore requirements further if necessary. Follow up with a documented version of the interview results and share those with the interviewee. Once interviewing has been completed, combine results with other elicitation activities.

Brainstorming

By bringing together a cross section of individuals across your stakeholder community you will get many different perspectives, and often the group will build on a single idea with the end result being particularly valuable learning. It's important to set the ground rules for a brainstorming session as this is where all ideas are welcome. It is not intended to evaluate or criticize ideas at this stage.

As with all of the elicitation methods, share the business objective and requirement evaluation criteria before starting. Ensure you have the means (e.g., note taker, whiteboard, flipcharts, etc.) and perhaps a process facilitator. Encourage people to explore and build off of ideas that have already been raised. After you've exhausted the idea pool, start the evaluation process. Run through the ideas and consolidate where appropriate. Ask the participants to raise pros and cons associated with the idea. Evaluate against the business objective(s) and the evaluation criteria established up front. Finish the effort with a commitment to document and publish to all participants.

Analysis of Current Tools

Take advantage of your stakeholder community to identify and collect examples of all existing documents, processes, and tools used in the general area of satisfying the business objectives. After collecting examples of each, review them to identify individual data elements being used and collected and the process steps being followed. Capture all separate inputs and outputs and then review to determine the requirements based on the combination of the two previous steps. Review the consolidation of requirements with the stakeholders to determine how each process or tool is used and accepted within the targeted user community. The final step is to document and share with all stakeholders.

Requirements Workshops

One of the most effective ways to identify requirements is a formal requirements workshop. The requirements workshop brings together representatives from each stakeholder group to have a facilitated discussion around the process of conducting win/loss reviews, and the resulting requirements. As with the other elicitation approaches, you should share the business objectives and other appropriate program documentation in advance of the workshop. Open the session with a discussion of the business objectives to ensure equal understanding among all participants. Through the process discussion, lead the identification of requirements and discuss as needed to ensure all appropriate feedback is collected and any potential issues have been identified. The final step is to review the process and the resulting requirements to obtain any final feedback. Resulting information should be combined into a single document and then shared with all stakeholder groups.

Surveys/Questionnaires

Conducting a survey among the various stakeholder communities is a great way to cover a broad range of people in a global setting. As with any survey, keep in mind that the response rate will be low (20% would be a great response rate), so you need to target a sufficiently high number of people.

In developing the survey, ensure you include both open and closed questions targeted toward addressing the business objective. The open questions require interpretation on the part of the project team and require analysis, so keep the open questions to a minimum. Identify the targeted stakeholders for the survey, making sure multiple people within each stakeholder community are targeted. You will likely need to send survey reminders out to increase your response rate.

When you have hit your survey deadline, collect the results and review the open-ended questions. Document the results and share with your stakeholders.

There are many survey tools available in the marketplace, so if your company does not have an infrastructure already in place you can easily find one to use. Of course you can also use tools like Word and Excel to conduct your survey.

Prototyping

Prototyping is an effective way to initiate the collection of requirements or to confirm requirements that have already been collected. With your list of requirements you can simply create a mockup of the actual process. This can be created using a variety of tools and does not have to work in terms of accepting data; it just has to convey the data elements that would be contained on the form and the general concepts behind the flow of information.

The mockup can be shared with stakeholders, but make sure you frame their review using the business goals and objectives originally established. Continue to iterate the mockup using feedback obtained from stakeholders and input from other elicitation activities. As you progress you can make a determination of when it's appropriate to create a working prototype. This can be created using the mockup tool or the software that will be used to create the final product.

This is a great tool to use to bring the requirements to life and can often elicit results that would not have been discovered otherwise.

Figure 9.1 illustrates the typical flow of activities associated with collecting and finalizing business requirements.

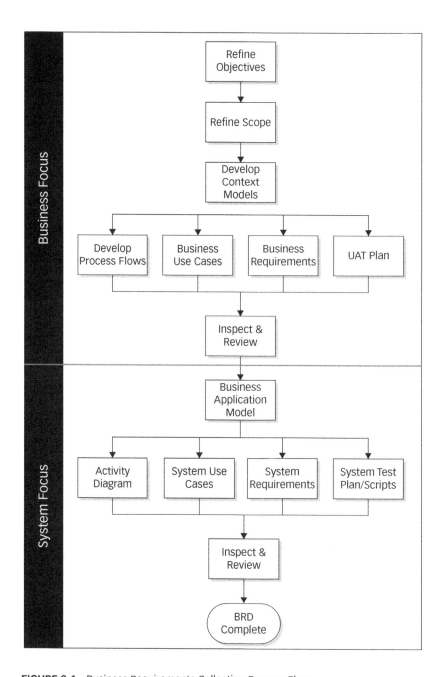

FIGURE 9.1 Business Requirements Collection Process Flow

As a reminder, the business goals and objectives must first be defined. Unless those are clearly stated up front and shared with all stakeholders prior to obtaining their feedback, the requirements gathered cannot truly be connected to meet the needs of the business.

GATHERING INSIGHTS FROM CURRENT TOOLS, PROCESSES, AND DOCUMENTS

The easiest way to start the requirements gathering process is to identify and obtain copies of processes, documents, or tools being used in pockets throughout the company to share competitive insights and conduct deal reviews. This can be done by creating a simple questionnaire and sharing it throughout the stakeholder communities previously identified. Specific areas to target include sales management, district and regional management, marketing, and competitive organizations within the company. Your questions within the survey should be structured to identify the following:

- What do they do?
  - General description of the activities surrounding the review and subsequent analysis of deal results.
  - Activities associated with publishing/sharing collateral that can be used by the sales teams to increase their success rates.
- Why do they do it?
  - Has the process been put in place to satisfy corporate reporting needs, is it used to identify deals that may be candidates for revival, or is it used to share knowledge and experience among the sales teams?
- Who is involved?
  - Who is tasked with providing the information—the input—to the process?
  - Who is responsible for managing the process?
  - Who collects the information and who uses it?

- How useful is the process?
  - Have they tracked results based on the process being followed and the information collected?
  - Has the process provided information that someone can take action on?
  - Does the information need further work before it can be consumed by the target audience?
- What tools do they use?
  - This could be a combination of commonly used software and communication tools, including email, Excel, Word, or PowerPoint.
  - It could also be rudimentary Web-based applications.
  - What modifications have been made to CRM systems to accommodate their business need?
  - Ask for copies or examples of, or access to, the tools being used and the reporting being conducted as a result of the information collected.
- What is the process and how it is implemented?
  - Ask for a process diagram or any document that describes how the process works.
  - Is the process standalone, or is it integrated into other processes?
  - Does the process need constant management, or does it run on its own?
- How do they use the information they collect?
  - Can they provide examples of how and where they have used the information collected?
  - Who is the target audience?
  - Does the information meet the needs of the business?

Using the results of the survey, compile a list of inputs and outputs and consolidate where possible to identify information consistent across the results.

IN-PERSON/GROUP INPUT

This input can be collected in a variety of ways, including in-person interviews, focus groups, brainstorming sessions, and requirements review sessions. Based on the list of stakeholders identified earlier, the project team should work together to determine the best elicitation method(s) to use and who they should use them with. For example, it may not be feasible to host a global brainstorming session, so you may need to engage the intended stakeholder audience with in-person interviews and surveys/questionnaires. Stakeholders within a reasonably close geographical location can be included in brainstorming or focus group sessions.

From the perspective of a win/loss review program, it's often useful to first split the stakeholders into two separate groups: corporate stakeholders and field stakeholders. Field stakeholders are defined as being directly or indirectly responsible for customer-related actions and activities. Corporate stakeholders are defined as either those responsible for the creation and publication of supporting material/programs to assist field stakeholders, or the product-development organizations responsible for the development and management of the company's products and services. Corporate stakeholders for a win/loss review program can also include investor relations and finance, as the information collected within the program can provide them with insight and guidance based on what is happening in the field on a day-to-day basis.

As identified earlier, the entry point to these elicitation activities must be the business goals and objectives. Without a clear understanding of the goals and objectives the stakeholders cannot frame their requirements and there is no ability to evaluate the merits of the requirements identified.

Each session or interview should function to gain understanding of the perspective of the participants, collect input from them relative to the data collection requirements and reporting requirements they would like to have satisfied, and then collate all results in a consistent format. We recommend structuring the elicitation activities so the following information is collected for each requirement:

- Requirement name and description
- Person/group initiating the requirement
- Business need being addressed
- Relative priority (as compared to other requirements identified within the session)
- Benefit to the organization if the requirement is satisfied

Through the collection of this information the project team will be in a position to consolidate all of the requirements identified, evaluate those requirements, and then communicate the results.

CONCERNS AND ISSUES

Throughout the elicitation phase, in addition to requirements being identified, issues and concerns will also be raised. Managing these issues and concerns as part of the overall project will help pave the way for global acceptance of the win/loss review program. Concerns will typically be raised along the following categories:

- Time commitment (from development right through implementation and field use)
- Funding
- Organizational readiness
- Implementation approach
- Long-term impact and acceptance

It is the responsibility of the project team in conjunction with the stakeholders to evaluate and develop a plan for addressing those concerns. For example, if the organizational culture does not accept failure (i.e., publication of a loss), one approach would be to allow for the anonymous submission of reviews.

CONSOLIDATION AND PUBLICATION OF RESULTS

As identified earlier, the creation of a BRD is an effective way to capture and share requirements with your stakeholders. Your company will likely have a standard format to follow, but if it does not, an easy Web search will present you with numerous templates you can use. The exact template isn't important. What is important is that a *single repository* lists the business objectives, stakeholders, and requirements. Future participants in the program can review the document so they can understand the history and the reasons specific decisions were made.

After you have completed the activities outlined earlier to identify business requirements, the final step is to consolidate and then publish. Consolidating business requirements is a straightforward (although time-consuming) task if you have captured the necessary information through your elicitation activities. All of the requirements are brought together in a single list and then reviewed for completeness. Any updates that are needed should be completed at this time. The next step is to group the requirements into categories and then to evaluate and remove duplicates if they exist. The resulting list is then structured to allow for a review based on the priorities. As you review and adjust priorities you will likely end up creating a series of releases, with a subset of the overall requirements being addressed in the first release and the remaining requirements addressed in future releases. This information can then be included in the BRD, and can be published and reviewed with stakeholders. It is important to document the rationale behind why requirements are addressed in a particular release versus a different one, as that information can then be clearly relayed to the stakeholders.

MANAGING PHASE

The final business requirements process phase is managing business requirements. This process phase begins once you obtain signoff on the business requirements artifact. The managing-requirements process is an ongoing one that occurs throughout the remainder of the project lifecycle. This is really just project change management specific to the business requirements. The process ensures that you enforce version control for any changes to the requirements. In this case, the term *changes* covers new requirements, changes to existing requirements, and the removal of existing requirements.

The process for change management is not unique to the implementation of a win/loss review program. As new requirements surface they should be evaluated against the overall goals and objectives as originally stated. In some cases, the goals and objectives themselves will change and so any requirements that have not yet been satisfied and any new requirements must be evaluated against these new objectives.

It's important to differentiate changes to business requirements from project scope changes, as they may be mutually exclusive decisions. The critical actions in this process phase include identifying changes, reviewing and assessing proposed changes, deciding to approve or reject proposed changes, and finally incorporating the changes into the applicable documentation and updating the overall plan.

DESIGN, DEVELOP, IMPLEMENT, AND SUPPORT

Each of the concepts of *design*, *develop*, *implement*, and *support* could have its own chapter. There are so many systems development life cycle (SDLC) choices available that it isn't feasible to cover them all. If you do not have a methodology that is supported within your company, then do a Web search on "Systems Development Life Cycle" and there will be a lot to choose from.

Particularly suited to the development and implementation of a win/loss review program is the *Agile development* method. There are many flavors of Agile development but each is predicated on multiple short release cycles that provide working software to individuals on a recurring basis, each new release targeting additional requirements and providing an opportunity for immediate feedback on the product as it is developed. An Agile development approach will allow you to get out in front of your stakeholder community with multiple versions they can feel and use, gaining their confidence and valuable input.

For the creation of a win/loss review program, the first step is to create a simple diagram that outlines the key components and major integration elements. (See Figure 9.2.) This doesn't have to be complicated, but it should cover the major input and output systems that have been identified through the requirements gathering process.

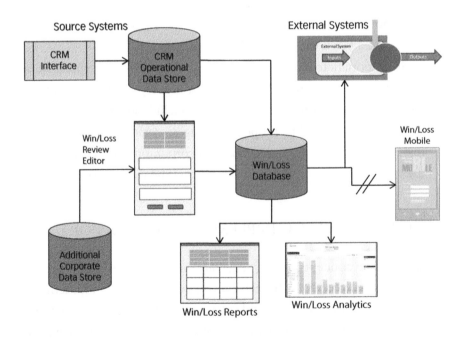

FIGURE 9.2 Data View of Win/Loss Review Process

Figure 9.2 can then be expanded to more closely document how the interfaces will work and the methods of communicating between each. At the same time the individual elements of the win/loss review program can be further designed. With the win/loss review editor there are typically three core functions that need to be planned for and documented. These include data to be displayed, data to be captured, and secondary actions to be taken. As we will be making multiple changes and modifications to the input form through the Agile development methodology, it's important to first establish a standard approach for each of the core functions. After the standard methodology is established, any modifications can be easily accommodated through that same standard approach. When the design has been completed, the coding can begin.

The results of the development activities can be shared with the stakeholders as they are ready. This interactive approach continues through the development until the primary requirements as identified have been addressed. Once completed, the first version can be shared with a selected target community to obtain user feedback. Based on the feedback the core components can be implemented for use with the entire stakeholder community.

Once the program is widely implemented, it will be necessary to have a user support structure in place to manage any issues and questions that arise. While great care may have been taken in gathering user requirements and system design, there will be several issues, questions, and new feature requests that arise. Perhaps a separate support team will be created to respond and interface with the field, while the development team focuses on the actual coding and testing of bug fixes and feature enhancements. This entire cycle continues as the program expands to address user input and the key requirements identified.

TRAINING AND GUIDANCE

As with most processes and programs that have broad user engagement and interactivity, some measure of user training is required to promote effective use of the process. For sellers to diligently and effectively perform win/loss reviews, they will need to learn this skill. You will recall from the preface that performing win/loss reviews is considered an advanced sales skill. If there is little or no documentation to help guide users toward self-sufficiency, they will likely become dissatisfied and frustrated with the process, ultimately undermining the program goals. Even the most intuitive program interface is not sufficient to guarantee success. Users also need to understand the bigger picture of where their contributions add value, and what value they will receive from their participation.

Several options exist for program training, and each has its advantages, characteristics, and level of sophistication suitable to the scale and complexity of the program and the capabilities of the organization to provide them.

Online User Guides

One of the simplest methods for user training is to provide online user guides. These are commonly constructed in the more popular user productivity software programs such as Microsoft Word and Microsoft PowerPoint, or in a popular portable document format such as Adobe Acrobat. There are many document formats to choose from and many document management and storage options. Typically, these will guide users through a sequential process covering the different features of the win/loss review tool. There will likely be a table of contents that users can reference to skip to a specific feature of the tool, as they may already be familiar with some aspects. For lengthy guides, it is important that sections are hyperlinked to facilitate navigation to and from the table of contents and other referenced sections.

As Web technologies evolve, there is a trend toward producing more interactive user guides that do not rely on a particular document format. Internal wiki-style document creation is quickly gaining favor among knowledge workers as it allows them to contribute to the training experience. It also allows content owners to publish updates in real time, becoming immediately available when the content is next accessed.

Screen Capture Videos

An effective method for software interface training is to create screen capture videos. Software programs such as Camtasia Studio® allow expert users to capture screen interactions with their program and record them as a *screencast*. There are many shareware programs offering similar capabilities, although with reduced feature sets. These screencasts can then be edited and enhanced with voiceovers and other effects to produce professional-looking user training videos.

An advantage of this content type is that it can be reused in many applications. It can be referenced, for example, in the previously mentioned wiki-style internal Web page, to be played as a streaming media file within a video frame or full-screen video player. Depending on the file size, it can also be attached in an email file. Many companies are moving toward cloud-based video streaming services such as YouTube and Screencast.com to host and deliver their internal video content in a secure and effective manner.

Interactive Online Training

A more sophisticated training program may include the creation of official curricula developed through the corporate training department. These training modules can be delivered in the formal training programs within a company, and perhaps be considered recommended or mandatory training, depending on the role. Although this may be a more expensive path, the interactive online training will likely be of very high quality and have a rich mixture of embedded video content, interactive demos, and knowledge checks to reinforce the learning along the way. To reinforce executive commitment, a program sponsor can be asked to record the opening and closing video segments and the reinforcing comments within. Completion of the online coursework can be tracked toward attainment of readiness goals. Training departments can solicit structured feedback and reviews to improve the content and delivery.

Workshops and Webinars

Workshops are an effective training method where a high degree of participant interactivity is designed into the training material, and where delivery is facilitated by a subject matter expert. Participants can work on real-world scenarios, perhaps using their own opportunities to conduct mock win/loss reviews that can be reviewed by peers and instructors. The lessons from these exercises, or even the outputs themselves, can be utilized in the actual win/loss reviews. This setting also offers a safe harbor to openly discuss perspectives, concerns, and issues. A printed classroom guide can be helpful where there is a lack of online connectivity or where attendees do not have their own laptops. It is recommended, however, that the size of paper documentation be minimized where possible, deferring the bulk of the content to online documentation.

The classroom workshop is usually the most expensive and time-consuming training model offered. Securing the time and budget commitments from participants is often the most challenging aspect as the workshops often require travel and lodging for those coming from distant offices. Another option to consider is the online workshop, or webinar, which can still offer several of the advantages of classroom delivery, but at a much reduced cost.

Audience participation may increase, but the person-to-person interactivity is greatly reduced. A webinar can also be recorded for future playback and be included as part of the overall training resources available.

SUMMARY

- Implementing a win/loss review process has characteristics similar to most other business processes that aim to deliver specific outputs to internal or external customers.
- To achieve the business goals of win/loss reviews, we adhere to the management discipline of BPM.
- The process owner for win/loss reviews is often a program director, business analyst, or process architect, and generally comes from the business side of the organization.
- The first action to be taken by the core win/loss review program team is to create the program goals and objectives.
- A formal project plan is critical to the success of company-wide deployment of the win/loss review process.
- The business requirements document is the publication of the collected business requirements to be satisfied by the program.
- The methods of collecting business requirements include interviewing, brainstorming, current tools analysis, requirement workshops, surveys, and prototyping.
- The Agile development method is an effective development approach for a win/loss review process.
- User training is an important component of program implementation, and several options exist to facilitate broad program training and adoption.

NOTE

1. International Institute of Business Analysis, *A Guide to the Business Analysis Body of Knowledge* (Toronto, Ontario, Canada: IIBA, 2009), p. 53. The IIBA's *BABOK Guide* outlines the process and tools associated with conducting elicitation activities for any given project.

CONCLUSION

A LOOK FORWARD

During the development of this book, I could not help but wonder how the practice of win/loss reviews would evolve over the next ten years. Perhaps the discipline of win/loss reviews will be widely incorporated as a logical step in the sales process model (and not necessarily the last step). As it stands today, there is even ambiguity over who owns or drives this discipline. Should it be part of the sales or marketing profession? Should it be part of operations? Perhaps the growing competitive intelligence profession will emerge as the clear thought leader and program champion.

The vision of futurists that information would be available at our fingertips is already being realized. Bill Gates, founder and chairman of Microsoft Corporation, foretold "a PC on every desktop and in every home." Although there remain several challenges to accessibility in many developing markets, many would agree that we have largely realized the essence of that vision.

One clear manifestation of that vision reflected throughout this book is the innovation wave referred to as the "consumerization of IT," characterized by an unprecedented range of information devices that enable near seamless connectivity between people and information. It also blurs the lines between work and personal life.

As these innovations make their way into the processes for collecting insights from our opportunity outcomes, it remains to be seen what additional paradigm shifts will occur when modes of speech, gesture, and other natural ways of interacting with and through our technology evolve. There are additional models and frameworks that are within reach today. For example, I envision a technology-driven process and framework that extends win/loss review collaboration and insights beyond the corporate firewalls and into the partner ecosystem. Consider the additional synergies gained when the partner channel and other intermediaries become contributors and beneficiaries in the knowledge model. Such knowledge sharing exists today, but it is usually through bilateral arrangement, not a multilateral matrix.

Perhaps by the time the sales opportunity reaches its win or loss stage, our systems will have done the reviews for us, having assimilated and analyzed yet-to-be-defined information sources. These reviews will still serve to inform the stakeholders after the fact, and may even form the basis for personalized learning programs that respond to the apparent skill or knowledge gaps. Recall our earlier discussion on the evolution of our BI systems that allow for user-defined reports and analytics. How we enhance our knowledge and skills will also target our specific needs.

But the real power will come when we incorporate the insights through predictive models that inform the sales teams and other stakeholders on the probability of outcomes, continuously updated as the opportunity progresses through the sales stages and as more information becomes available. As these models are predictive, the seller can model the effect that the *mix* of various factors will have on the outcome.

While we await the arrival of the future, there are plenty of opportunities today to innovate and explore how and where win/ loss reviews benefit businesses of all shapes and sizes. Although most of this book has focused on a seller-oriented process, there are many models available today that can be implemented to address your company's specific needs and orientation. Like a well-balanced investment portfolio, a blend of approaches will yield healthy insights without the inherent risks or faults of a single approach. The businesses that survive and thrive in the coming decades will be those that have mastered of the art and science of win/loss reviews. I hope that yours will be among them.

PROCESS IMPROVEMENT: A CASE STUDY

This case study evaluates the process and methodologies used in certifying the win/loss review process as a Six Sigma Black Belt project at Microsoft Corporation. It shares the insights gained from a process improvement perspective but does not cover broader benefits and results, such as improvements in win rates or revenue performance. The outcomes will vary by company or organization, but it is hoped that discussing the key elements and lessons learned from this process here will assist process owners and consultants who are contemplating the implementation of new in-house win/loss review processes or improving upon an existing one. There are many tools and methods available for a process improvement project, and many were used for this project. For brevity and relevance, only the actual methods and tools employed for this project from the Six Sigma discipline are explored. To respect confidential and proprietary data, actual values have been modified or removed.

BACKGROUND

As with many businesses, Microsoft's ability to earn revenue and grow value for its shareholders is largely dependent on how well it grows opportunities and manages its sales pipeline, with the obvious intent to win opportunities at a profit. And like many businesses, Microsoft offers multiple product and service lines and operates in a highly competitive marketplace where most opportunities will have their corresponding competitor offerings going after the same piece of business.

While it was a fairly simple exercise to discover who the sales teams were competing against in any given opportunity, and to assess who they were winning and losing against (the *what*), the sparse competitive intelligence from the field sales teams was making it difficult for the business to understand the impact of competitive forces on opportunity outcomes (the *why*). To complicate matters, an additional outcome classification, "disengage," was used as a convenient alternative to what might have otherwise been either a loss or a potential win that was walked away from too soon. Other organizations may refer to this by other names: "no-decision," "deactivated," "suspended," "unforecasted," and so on. This practice often masked developing risks and created competitive blind spots, which made corrective actions difficult and strategic resource planning more challenging. Further, there was no consistent and integrated method, tool, or process for conducting, collecting, managing, and analyzing win/loss reviews on a worldwide basis.

PROBLEM STATEMENT

Perhaps to some extent the practice at Microsoft where field leaders *own* their business often disconnected processes and practices from what was provided as a centralized process. Field sales teams often had their own win/loss review process utilizing a myriad of technologies and strategies. Many focused only on reviewing losses, while others favored wins. Although a central win/loss review process was in place for several years, its relatively low adoption rate by the field sales teams, measured as a percentage of opportunities reviewed out of the total opportunities won, lost, or disengaged, provided marginal value for corporate stakeholders. The problem, therefore, was not so much that there was low utilization; it was that the prior process was built to serve the needs of our corporate stakeholders while treating the sales teams as merely the information gatherers. Although the information captured had some value for the local teams, surfacing insights useful to other sales teams and stakeholders such as the product and marketing group was also marginal in value.

HYPOTHESIS

It was hypothesized that the implementation of a global standard for conducting win/loss reviews that focused primarily on the needs of front-line sellers (versus corporate stakeholders) would provide the compelling experience for collecting, analyzing, and disseminating actionable insights on a real-time basis. This effectively made the sales teams the primary customer. It was further posited that significant efficiencies would be realized, and a stronger value chain created, by unifying or linking several business processes that utilized essentially the same source data, eliminating process redundancies, and improving business decision making.

APPROACH

Microsoft elected to solve the problem utilizing *Six Sigma*, an internationally recognized discipline for continuous process improvement commonly found in manufacturing and product development disciplines. Under Microsoft's Quality and Business Excellence (QBE) program, the team responsible for the win/loss review project utilized the Plan, Deliver, Operate (PDO) framework as the process improvement approach advocated and supported by the QBE organization.

As referenced in Figure A.1, the PDO framework maps directly to the five primary phases of Six Sigma: *define, measure, analyze, improve,* and *control* (DMAIC). The Project Charter contained the high-level outline of the business case, problem statement, project goals, outputs, baseline metric definition, team members, sponsors and champions, and scope of the project. For this project, a *defect* was defined as any qualified opportunity that reached win, loss, or disengage status that was over a certain value but that did not get recorded in the global win/loss review tool within 30 days from the time its status changed to "win," "loss," or "disengage."

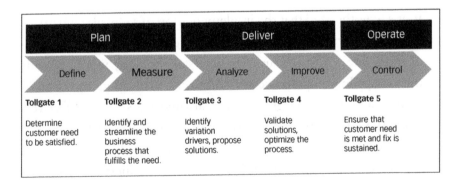

FIGURE A.1 Stages of Six Sigma Aligned with PDO Framework

DEFINE PHASE

In the *define* phase the team wanted to first establish the business case and have leadership support on the issue that needed to be addressed. To create the business case, several weeks of research were conducted to determine how win/loss reviews were being conducted, what information they provided, and who the primary beneficiaries were. Further research was conducted to determine the amount of rigor being applied to understanding major wins and losses and where this information was surfacing. It was also known at the time that there were a high number of disengaged opportunities, but little evidence to show the real competitive vulnerabilities underlying those opportunities. After finalizing the business case and getting approval to deliver the project, the team had to understand what the customers wanted and how they were linked to the problem. In the define phase the project team utilized many project management tools to ensure not only that the Six Sigma project would be successful from an analysis perspective, but also that it would be managed to a specific timeline with limited resources and a tight budget.

VOICE OF THE CUSTOMER

As discussed earlier, the field sales teams were now the customer in this process. Therefore, understanding what the field sales teams wanted from a win/loss review process was the first order of business. Capturing the *voice of the customer* (VoC) was done by implementing a company-wide survey of individuals in particular roles who would own specific opportunities—primarily the account managers and sales specialists. The project team created a survey of roughly 15 questions. Each one of the questions was thoroughly analyzed to ensure that responses were relevant and actionable.

This allowed the team to minimize the number of questions while maintaining the integrity of the survey and the results. This also reduced the amount of time needed for each participant to complete the survey. The survey was conducted using an internal survey tool and distributed to over 1,500 people, with a response rate of nearly 200 respondents, or 13%.

Figure A.2 summarizes some of the verbatim responses from the internal survey.

The survey results were then translated into what are referred to as *critical to quality* (CTQ) elements, such as quick capture, easy reporting, and global access. Using a Kano model (see Figure A.3), further refinements to the survey results allowed the identification of *hygiene elements*, or elements that are considered expected, and *delighters*, or elements that would improve customer satisfaction beyond those that are considered critical. In this case, the customers are defined as the members of field sales teams.

Once the CTQs were identified in the Kano tool, further analysis was completed on the hygiene factors and CTQs that were to be addressed. Care was taken to ensure that each CTQ was measurable and quantifiable. To do this the project team went back to

---

Summarized Verbatims from Win-Loss Review Field Survey

- "Access to win/loss learnings from other subsidiaries."
- "Need a consolidated reporting system."
- "Need tight integration with our CRM and other reporting tools."
- "Report win/loss trends and best/worst practices quarterly and yearly."
- "Report to someone empowered to act on trends causing us to lose deals."
- "Consolidate all losses and wins in a single report."
- "Make it automatic as part of every opportunity."
- "Much more transparency is needed for both wins and losses."

FIGURE A.2   Voice of the Customer Survey Responses

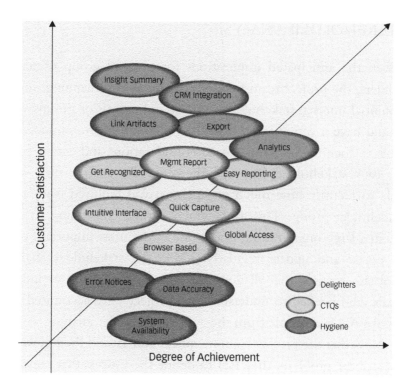

FIGURE A.3 Kano Model Translating VoC into CTQ Elements

a smaller group of customers and asked specific questions about each CTQ and what success would look like. After consolidating the feedback, team members were able to create metrics for each CTQ. These metrics became the key performance indicators (KPIs) for measuring the performance of the win/loss review process. This allowed them to establish goals and measure progress toward those goals based on their customer's requirements. For instance, "easy reporting" was further defined to be only three clicks to a report result, whereas "quick capture" was defined as allowing input of a win/loss review in less than 10 minutes. These quantifiable CTQs now allowed them to measure what the customer wanted and allowed them to establish process goals.

STAKEHOLDER ANALYSIS

Given the anticipated implications for a broad group of stake-holders, the project team focused its energies on mapping out all potential internal stakeholders—those individuals or groups who would have a vested interest in the outcomes of the project—as well as documenting any special considerations and action plans for each stakeholder. Through the *stakeholder analysis* they were able to identify how much engagement was required from each stakeholder group. This tool, which is time consuming to create in a large organization, is also one of the most important ones to create and update regularly. Using the stakeholder analysis tool also ensured that all impacted stakeholder groups or individuals who needed to understand the project were accounted for. Figure A.4 is a sample from the actual stakeholder analysis.

Now that the project team members understood their customers and the problem, they had to define the process that contributed to the problem. A high-level process map (see Figure A.5) and an internal communications plan were also developed during this phase. The high-level process map is a flowchart of the *as-is* process that has little detail but clearly defines the start and end points of the win/loss review process and gives a high-level view of the process steps. This was critical to clearly communicate with the project team on what was in scope and out of scope for this project. As more was learned about the current state, a more detailed as-is process map was created and used in later phases.

With our stakeholder analysis completed, the engagement method for each stakeholder was now understood and the communication plan developed. The *communication plan* is a tool used to identify the message, frequency, medium, and owner of communications inside and outside of the project team. Individuals were categorized into communication buckets that defined the various communication parameters, which ranged from minimum

Stakeholder	Considerations	Action Plan
Field Sales (Account Managers, Sales Specialists)	• Improve competitive capabilities without taxing selling time • Motivated by recognition and increasing sales • Timid about sharing loss information	• Regularly communicate easily consumed competitive insights based on peer inputs • Ensure that recognition is core messaging component • Link with rewards/incentives program
Sales Leadership	• Focused on transactions; have no automated process for rolling up and identifying competitive threats	• Ensure win-loss forms part of Sales Leadership curriculum program (i.e., Microsoft Sales Academy)
Role Owners	• Focus on talent transformation through coaching and self-assessments • Short window to influence updated performance assessment tools	• Review all past and planned Profiles of Excellence to be part of Excellence Indicators • Plan global incentive program launched through role owners
Sales Operations Leads	• Streamlining processes by integrating data sources to inform forecasts and BI • Emphasis on enablement but with more inspection of performance • Core stakeholder for landing in field	• Work with Area SE leads for implementing local landing plans for Areas and Subsidiaries • Leverage and showcase early trials and seller references
Compete Leads	• Competitive forces in field taking greater share, need to empower local leads with actionable intelligence	• Contribute regularly to CMSG Compete monthly communiqué
Enterprise Marketing	• High energy and costs expended in finding and documenting customer case studies from disparate sources • Systems not integrated as part of natural sales motion	• Communicate value to WW CEP leads for increasing case study leads

FIGURE A.4 Stakeholder Analysis

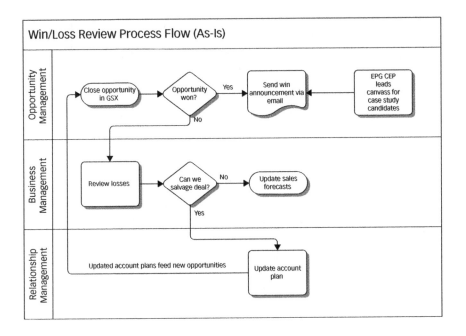

Win/Loss Review Process Flow (As-Is)

FIGURE A.5   High-Level As-Is Process Map

updates to very engaged and detailed communications. With the creation of the communication plan, the vehicles of communication were identified and assigned to the various buckets to ensure effective and relevant communication to all stakeholders. Several communication vehicles were employed, ranging from major launch campaigns at the annual sales meeting to monthly communication letters and weekly updates. A series of "how-to" and promotional videos were also produced. These broad communications allowed the project team to address the needs of stakeholders, obtain their feedback, and sustain their buy-in and support of the enhanced win/loss process.

The project team identified early that the development and execution of a communication plan was critical to the success of the project, and referenced the Kotter model[1] (see Figure A.6) as

1	**Establish a Sense of Urgency** ▪ Examine market and competitive realities. ▪ Identify and discuss crises or major opportunities.
2	**Form a Powerful Guiding Coalition** ▪ Assemble a group with enough power to lead the change effort. ▪ Encourage the group to work together as a team.
3	**Develop a Clear Vision** ▪ Create a vision to help direct the change effort. ▪ Develop strategies for achieving that vision.
4	**Share the Vision and the Need for Change** ▪ Use every vehicle possible to communicate the new vision and strategies. ▪ Teach new behaviors by the example of the guiding coalition.
5	**Empower Others to Act on the Vision** ▪ Eliminate obstacles to change. ▪ Change systems or structures that seriously undermine the vision. ▪ Encourage risk taking and nontraditional ideas, activities, and actions.
6	**Plan for and Create Short-Term Wins** ▪ Plan for visible performance improvements. ▪ Create those improvements. ▪ Recognize and reward employees involved in the improvements.
7	**Consolidate improvements** ▪ Leverage increased credibility to change systems & policies that don't fit the vision. ▪ Hire, promote, and develop employees who can implement the vision. ▪ Reinvigorate with new projects, themes, and change agents.
8	**Institutionalize the Change** ▪ Articulate the connections between the new behaviors and corporate success. ▪ Develop the means to ensure leadership development and succession.

FIGURE A.6   Kotter Model

a key change-management guide and tool. As with any Six Sigma project, change management is usually the most challenging part of the project. The change management process was started early and was driven proactively throughout the life cycle of the project.

MEASURE PHASE

Once the project team finalized the CTQs and the KPIs, it was time to start collecting data from the current process. The team members wanted to ensure accurate and complete data that was worthy of being analyzed. Since they had clear process goals (KPIs), they were able to create a data collection plan that was based on those KPIs. In the data collection plan they clarified operational definitions of each metric and how they were going to collect the data. Once they had enacted the data collection plan and collected the data, they completed a *measurement system analysis* (MSA). An MSA ensures that the data is both repeatable and reproducible, allowing the team to ensure the data is worthy of analysis. This MSA was performed to evaluate the actual win/loss reviews conducted against the total number of opportunities that reached their final stages. To complete the MSA, two separate teams collected data. They then compared the data that each team received to ensure a successful MSA and confirmed that the data was of high quality. This was an important step to ensure that the measurement systems were sound and that statistical analysis could be conducted with a high level of confidence.

Once the MSA was completed, the team was able to assess how the process was performing and to see process behavior changes throughout the year and year over year. These behavior changes could be addressed and understood in the next phase.

Since the project team was dealing with attribute data for the win/loss reviews where the item was either defective or not defective, the team members utilized the Binomial Process Capability of Defects analysis from Minitab to evaluate their current process capability. It indicated a sigma (σ) value of less than 1 on a worldwide basis, with varying σ values when parsed by different geographical regions. This allowed the project team to understand the current state process and provided the baseline for the process. Having this information clarified how large their goal was.

ANALYZE PHASE

In the *analyze* phase, the team set out to identify areas that could have been causing process defects. To quickly do this and generate some theories they created a *fishbone diagram* (see Figure A.7) to understand the causes and effects of the current state process. To complete this tool the team members received input (through brainstorming) from the subject matter experts and were able to develop potential causes, or x's in the metaphorical equation: $y = f(x_1) + f(x_2) + f(x_3) \ldots$, where y is the defect. Once the fishbone was created the team members prioritized the potential causes (x's). They now had a list of prioritized potential causes around which they were able to develop theories. This same diagram was useful for focusing on a few areas suspected of causing the majority of the defects. Other potential causes were useful in the development of the control plan.

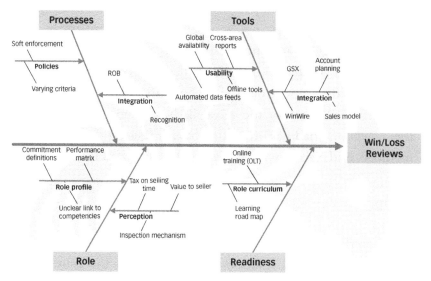

FIGURE A.7   Fishbone Diagram Used to Brainstorm Potential x's

Several potential correlating and causal factors were reviewed and hypotheses developed and tested. These tests were focused on the process itself, not on the causal relationship of the factors selected in the win/loss reviews.

The first hypothesis focused on whether the win/loss process integration into the sales review cycle had an effect on the process performance. After running a series of 2-Sample % Defective tests among different regions, it was determined that there was insufficient evidence to conclude that the level of sales process integration impacted win/loss performance. This did not mean that it was not a factor, only that there was not enough evidence to reject the hypothesis.

Another hypothesis focused on whether the opportunity outcome had an effect on whether win/loss reviews were completed for a given opportunity. A Chi-square % Defective test was utilized and the conclusion was that there were differences in the defects related to the opportunity outcome. "Loss" outcomes were more likely to have a win/loss review completed. This finding was consistent with earlier feedback that suggested that win/loss reviews were being used as an inspection mechanism to assist with opportunity review meetings, not as a beneficial function for the field sales teams to learn and apply the insights.

The team completed other hypothesis tests based on the other root causes that came from the fishbone diagram. Now that they had identified some of the most likely and potential causes for the defects and had performed hypothesis tests on them, the team members understood what needed to be improved in next phase.

IMPROVE PHASE

Based on the team's analysis, another brainstorming session helped to generate potential solutions for each one of the root causes.

After a selection of the best solutions was finalized, a new win/loss review process was created that would address the CTQs and root causes. This included CTQs such as time to input, reporting efficiency, and global access. Once the new application was built and operational, the team performed a pilot prior to a full rollout of the new application. To ensure a successful pilot the team updated the process map, responsibility matrix (RACI), and documentation of the new process.

The formal pilot project was executed within one of 13 regions to test a new sales model and process design. The new design focused on moving the win/loss review activity closer to the point at which the opportunity was closed out in the CRM. Whereas before the process depended largely on whether the opportunity was a loss, it was now implemented as a standard part of the final sales stage regardless of the outcome. Figure A.8 illustrates where the process enhancements were focused.

Win/loss reviews were also implemented as a standard agenda item in the monthly sales reviews for wins, losses, and disengaged opportunities. This was an important adoption by sales managers as it clearly communicated that win/loss reviews were an expected part of the sales review process and that the reporting function of the win/loss review process would be the only reference for sales reviews.

Finally, to counter the perception that win/loss reviews were only for losses and for inspecting sales outcomes, the win/loss review process served as a prerequisite for recognition programs and general recognition emails. Integration with these programs meant that the information would automatically feed into these systems, eliminating the manual reentry of information.

After running a 2-Sample % Defective test of the data from the pilot region (see Figure A.9), it was determined that the pilot yielded strong evidence to implement the improvements on a

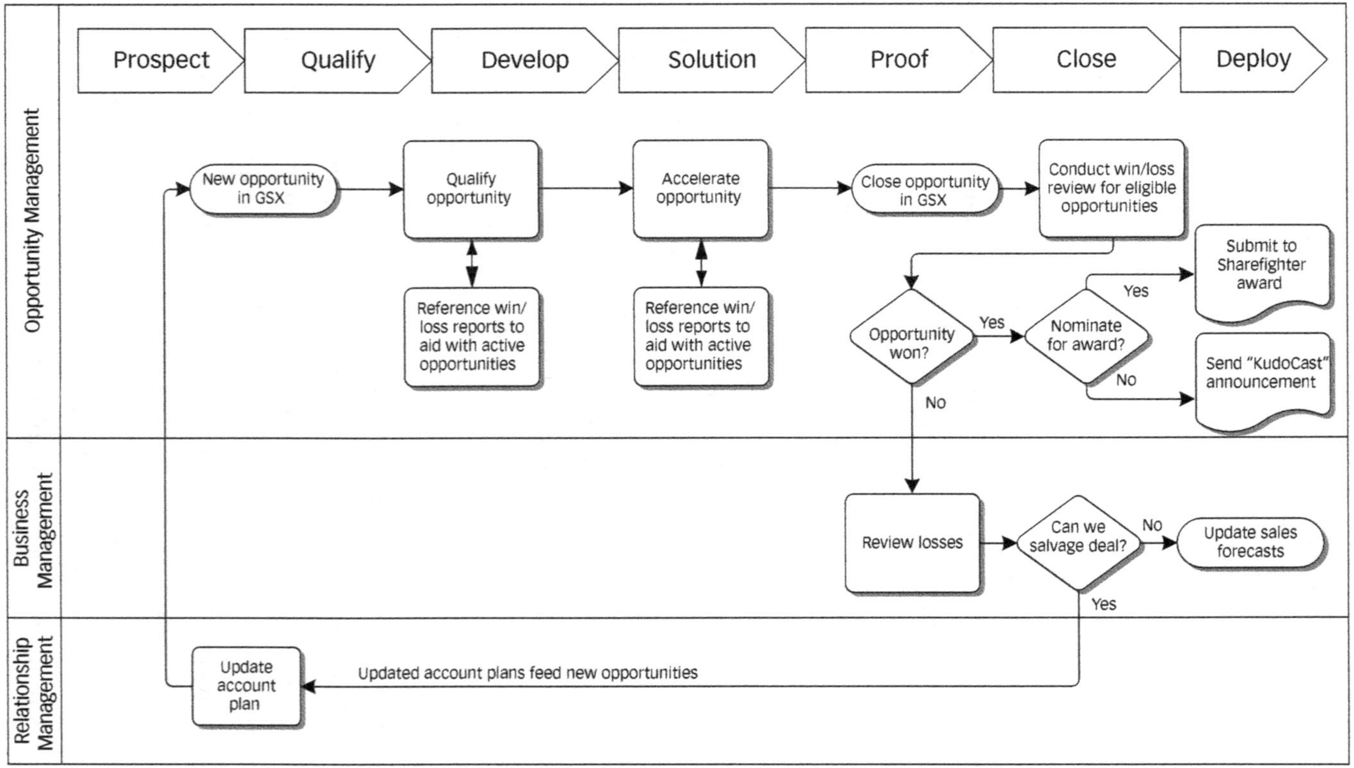

FIGURE A.8 "To Be" Process Map

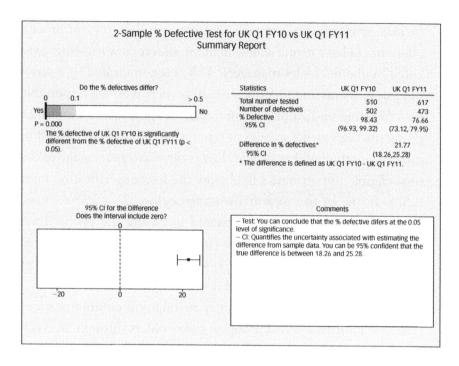

FIGURE A.9 Statistical Confirmation of the Results from the Pilot Study

global scale. The data showed a clear statistical improvement in the region where the pilot was performed.

The global rollout plan was created based on specific characteristics of each region. This allowed the team to prioritize the regions to enable an efficient and successful global rollout. Based on the success of the pilot, the team was able to use those benefits and share them with each region as the business case. This allowed the executives of each region to understand and adopt the new application with their field teams to record their win/loss reviews.

CONTROL PHASE

To ensure that the new process would remain within control, the team created and documented a control plan. The *control plan* focuses primarily on ensuring that the win/loss review process continues to have strong adoption in the sales review meetings executed by the field sales managers. This is accomplished by a series of measurements and identification of owners who are responsible for collecting and displaying the data. To guarantee compliance on the measurements a series of reports and alerts were created to show when the number of win/loss reviews as a percentage of the total eligible opportunities fell below the lower specification limit (LSL). If one of the measurements fell below the control limits, then an escalation plan was activated to ensure the proper level of attention to address the issue. In addition, the internal portal homepage posts comparative KPIs with a crawl showing the most recent win/loss reviews entered into the system.

Augmenting the control plan is an ongoing communications plan that informs a broad group of stakeholders through an email newsletter as to how the field is using the win/loss review process, the insights gained, and best practices to share.

RESULTS

The resulting benefits of a well-tuned win/loss review program are numerous and significant. As this case study focused on reducing the defects as defined earlier, the level of win/loss review process adoption as measured by the sigma level improved by over 2σ in less than one year! This essentially means that there is nearly universal adoption of the win/loss review process on a global scale, and that it is largely driven by the front-line sellers who recognize the value to their sales efforts, not only for themselves but for the broader stakeholder community.

Enhancements were made to the existing process, and the tool itself was further enhanced by creating four different modules, or subsections, that serve specific functions and target audiences (see Figure A.10). The modularity allows for system enhancements, testing, and maintenance without affecting the entire process. This was also consistent with the Agile development model that allowed for step iterations and rapid prototyping and deployment.

In summary, through the Six Sigma methodology the team was able to utilize a structured way to address and solve its business problem. It focused on what was critical to the customer and developed the relevant measures to track progress. Indeed, it helped the team define who the customer was. After the team understood the goals, current process, and metrics, it was able to perform a root-cause analysis and verify the vital few root causes. This enabled the team to develop the best solutions to address each root cause and incorporate them into the solution that was piloted. After a successful pilot the team was able to create the rollout plan for the

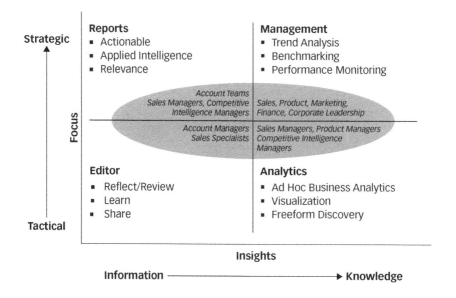

FIGURE A.10 Four Modules of the Win/Loss Review Process at Microsoft

other regions and start the broader implementation. Through this whole process the team spent a considerable amount of time and energy on the change management aspect to ensure that the new process was received and adopted by each region.

NOTE

1. J. Kotter, *Leading Change: Why Transformation Efforts Fail* (Boston: Harvard Business School Press, 1995).

APPENDIX B

FROM THE
BLOGOSPHERE

On many Internet forums there exists lively debate and discussion around the topic of win/loss reviews. Discussions occur in many types of sites—professional networks, competitive intelligence, product management, and even dedicated topic sites. Many professionals host their own blogs and invite commentary from interested parties. Here, our goal is to expose the wide range of opinions around the topic and its numerous dimensions that are captured in Internet forums and blogs. While this book does indeed advocate an informed position on various aspects and approaches, it is in the spirit of learning that we reflect on the ongoing dialogue harvested from the public discourse. As copyright law is yet unclear on the ownership rights of posted opinions on various social networking sites, we have elected to summarize the discussion threads while preserving the intent of the posts.

ON WHETHER SALES TEAMS OR CUSTOMER INTERVIEWS PROVIDE MOST INSIGHTS

In one Internet forum a user asked whether account managers or customers provide the best feedback for win/loss reviews. In researching the most accurate and least biased way of collecting insights from win/loss reviews, there are a few schools of thought as to the best way to go about this. Many will completely dismiss the seller's perspective as inherently biased (she lost because of price; he won because of his great relationship skills). Most will say that it is the customer's voice that matters most. However, don't customers have biases, too? Who runs the review: sales or marketing? And do we engage the services of a third party with the assumption that we're eliminating bias? What role do social media play? And do we look at going narrow but deep, or broad and not-so-deep?

The customer often has a better perspective on why a company did *not* win the deal, whereas the sales team might be better able to explain why they *won* the deal. The problem arises when a loss review is left up to the sellers, in which case they will often offer excuses instead of making an objective analysis, and often do not take accountability for the loss. This is a common perception held by many forum participants. In addition, the sales team may not even know the real reason for the win or loss. And taking accountability and owning up to the loss might lead to their termination.

Other positions were more directed at strategic accounts, where it was often discussed that with these accounts there should never be a loss, especially if there were only pricing issues. To a point this might be true, but we cannot dismiss an account as not being strategic just because pricing was an issue. There are often many deals in a strategic account, and not all of them will be won. Think of when your own company might be a strategic account to a supplier. These relationships usually exist on a higher level than just price. But you may still bargain with your supplier, and in some cases reject their offer if there is not enough value to justify the price. This, however, does not mean that you are not a strategic account to this supplier.

EFFECT OF SOCIAL NETWORKING ON WIN/LOSS REVIEWS

The penetration of social networking and social media is changing the dialogue toward more transparency. Indeed, one can argue that the discourse is becoming less civil in tone as the cloak of anonymity protects the person opining. Even where anonymity is not provided, the nature of the dialogue is more open and direct, partly due to the need to keep communications contained in short bursts. There is a trend observed over the past three or so years that sellers are becoming more accountable for, or at least more self-critical of, their wins and losses. As the younger generations are making their way into business professions, they are more open to adopting the engagement paradigms of social media, where their opinions are more openly expressed, often with the expectation that many hundreds of their peers will also be consuming their opinions.

The effect that this is having on the internal business dialogue is that lofty praise and unproductive blame are noticeably shifting toward objective reflection of individual and team performance. But it was also argued that there will always be biases even as we engage in more open discourse, regardless of whether the reviews are done by the sales teams or by a neutral third party. The value, it seems, is that over time the wisdom improves as deals are reviewed, regardless of the outcome. As more information becomes available, the ability to create knowledge improves.

WHAT WIN/LOSS REVIEWS MAY REVEAL BEYOND PRICING ISSUES

In many blogs and forums, pricing and product issues were commonly referenced as the primary factors related to wins and losses. It was observed that the apparent level of customer engagement experience and complexity of the sale greatly influenced these discussions. In many cases the amount of factors depended on the industry and vertical. Some highly specialized industries had unique factors, but most of them had a common set of high-level factors.

Competitive differentiation was cited most often after pricing and product as an influencing factor. This was especially true with the larger and more strategic accounts where the business is so competitive that the outcomes are often decided on very narrow criteria, or criteria that have all but discarded price and product. These differentiators are quite important to senior leadership as they can be exploited at several levels (e.g., marketing campaigns, brand perceptions, etc.). The perception of competitive differentiation often depends on how well a company manages its customer evidence, such as having references and case studies.

Channel partners were also frequently discussed as a key influence on the outcome. Win/loss reviews will look at the extent to which partner support played a role. When discussing an account base requiring high-complexity solutions, a specialized channel was often mentioned as a primary factor. Win/loss reviews were quite effective, and often cited as a mechanism for revealing the capability gaps in the channel.

One of the benefits often cited is that seller-oriented win/loss reviews provide a lot of ready material that can help with the formulation of the account plan. Accessing the aggregated insights from past win/loss reviews provides ideas for further opportunity development, business need and solution alignment, and competitive profiling. Several forums mentioned that sales teams give credibility to the insights that come from other sellers or from others whom they know. This can often lead to better execution of the tactics and strategies in an account plan.

WIN/LOSS REVIEW PROCESS IMPROVEMENT

I recently completed a Six Sigma Black Belt project focused on our win/loss review process. I had been running this program for about two years when I decided to put a bit of scientific rigor behind it. It was a six-month program that defined a defect (y) as an opportunity that met certain criteria and that did not get a win/loss review completed. There can be many defects in a process with a high amount of human involvement. That simple defect definition gave us a starting point that made us look long and hard at all potential x's in the equation $y = f(x_1) + f(x_2) + f(x_3) \ldots$

Without going through each phase of DMAIC (*define, measure, analyze, improve,* and *control*), I can tell you that the four key areas I feel were most helpful in the process were the voice of the customer (VoC) translated to CTQs, stakeholder analysis, the communication plan, and the control plan. Another strategy that worked out well was focusing on a single geography for the pilot plan, and then scaling the lessons through the *improve* phase. The relatively low impact that you are experiencing may be due to your wanting to boil the ocean. Take a piece of the business and nurture it to the point that you see the results you're looking for. In my case, I was able to use the pilot geography to influence the rest of the business with practices that are producing verifiable results.

A key differentiator that we used was to focus on seller-driven win/loss reviews. Nearly everyone I know dismisses the seller's insights. But when we designed a process that allowed sellers to capture in 15 minutes their insights from opportunities that were won, lost, or disengaged, they were able to stick to the relevant insights of the opportunity. We also designed it in such a way that the insights cascaded throughout the organization, aggregating the information and exposing it at the right altitudes, depending on the audience. And by linking the process to recognition systems, we got the sellers to deposit their knowledge for wins before getting broader recognition. Further, the system was designed to recycle their knowledge back to them so they could use it for their active opportunities.

Because our process places equal weight on the insights from reviewing both wins and losses, there is a neutral position, meaning that people will not necessarily be rewarded or punished for these insights. It's definitely a cultural shift, but in a learning organization where the corporate leadership supports continuous improvement, uncovering errors is less of an issue. We learn from them.

The process we designed has since been institutionalized worldwide. While pockets of resistance remain, it continues to gain broad stakeholder support and interest.

APPENDIX C

SOFTWARE AND SERVICES FOR WIN/ LOSS REVIEW

SOFTWARE SOLUTION

The win/loss review framework is technology agnostic. Following is a detailed list of technologies used for the solution implemented at Microsoft.

Server and Database Technology
- ADOMD.net (Data access to SSAS)
- Windows Communications Foundation (Web services used between win/loss application and all data sources)
- Microsoft SQL Server 2008 R2 (DB, SSIS, SSAS)
- Microsoft Windows Server 2008

Application Technology
- CSS
- HTML
- JavaScript
- JQuery
- Microsoft .NET 4.0
- Microsoft Active Directory
- Microsoft ASP.NET
- Microsoft Exchange Server
- Microsoft IIS 7
- Microsoft Office 2010
- Microsoft Silverlight 4
- Microsoft Silverlight Pivot Viewer
- Microsoft Visual Studio 2010
- Sysgain Collection Designer
- Telerik RadControls for Silverlight

Mobile Technology
- GhostScript
- Microsoft Visual Studio 2010
- Microsoft Windows Phone 7
- Microsoft Windows Phone 7 SDK

PARTNER PROFILES

The following technology partners were involved in the development of the win/loss review process.

The Grasp Group

The Grasp Group is a consulting firm specializing in solving enterprise business challenges through experienced program management and subject matter expertise. They are the overall program

managers and development leads of the win/loss review program at Microsoft.
Contact: Steve Puchala
Email: spuchala@winloss.com
Web: www.winloss.com

Sysgain

Sysgain is a Microsoft Partner focused on software and mobile solutions development and consulting for Fortune 500 customers. Sysgain focuses on their Web development, SQL, SharePoint, and Windows Phone 7 expertise to deliver both the desktop and mobile platforms that support the entire program.
Contact: Michael Brophy
Email: mbrophy@sysgain.com
Web: www.sysgain.com

Decisive Data

Decisive Data focuses on delivering decision-making insight for customers through business intelligence, data warehousing, OLAP analytics, and innovative data visualizations. Decisive Data has combined information from the win/loss review program with detailed sales opportunity information from the global CRM system to provide competitive trending and actionable insights.
Contact: Luke Hartsock
Email: luke@decisivedata.net
Web: www.decisivedata.net

GLOSSARY

Account manager The person responsible for managing the day-to-day activities and relationship of a customer account with the purpose of facilitating and managing the sale of a product and/or service.

Account plan A documented artifact and process intended to align and address customer and business priorities in order to map products and solutions to those needs.

Agile software development Agile software development is a group of software development methodologies based on iterative and incremental development, where requirements and solutions evolve through collaboration between self-organizing, cross-functional teams.

Analyze phase The phase in Six Sigma quality improvement methodology where current performance is evaluated against future requirements.

App   Abbreviation of the word *application*; commonly refers to an application designed to run on any mobile device, or a lighter version of a fully featured application (e.g., applet).

Bias   The subjective influence that a person can impose on the recording of facts related to opportunity outcomes.

Bimodal   The dual state characteristic of factors related to win/loss reviews, where the same factor can be attributed for a positive or negative outcome (win or loss).

Bluebird   An unexpected and often high-value sale that was closed without having been managed or forecasted by the sales team.

Boolean search   Common with most search engines, the use of logical operators such as AND, OR, and NOT in freeform text searches that aims to improve the relevance and precision of search results.

Brainstorming   A group creativity technique where participants are encouraged to explore all ideas without preestablished constraints, designed to generate a large number of ideas for the solution to a problem.

Business intelligence (BI)   The business insights enabled by information technology that allow structured and ad hoc query of correlated data and turn it into actionable information. BI is particularly powerful when able to aggregate multiple data sources and present them in a way that facilitates planning and strategic decision making.

Business process management (BPM)   An IT-enabled discipline that promotes organizational agility and supports efforts of managers to drive process change and rapid innovation to better meet internal customer requirements and expectations.

Business requirements document (BRD)   Documents the details of the business solution for a project, including customer needs and expectations. The BRD process can be incorporated within a Six Sigma define, measure, analyze, improve, and control (*DMAIC*) project.

Causal correlation The effect that one factor has on another, such that the relationships are not merely correlated.

Communication plan A discipline used to identify the message, frequency, medium, and owner of a communication inside and outside of the project team.

Competitive factors Any factor in the competitive category affecting the outcome of an opportunity. These can relate to, but are not limited to, differentiation and references.

Competitive intelligence (CI) The discipline of gathering, analyzing, and distributing intelligence about products, customers, competitors to support a broad set of stakeholder objectives.

Consultative selling An inquiry-led sales process where sellers assist buyers in clearly understanding their business needs, guiding them through the buying process.

Consumerization of IT The growing influence that consumer experiences with IT (e.g., consumer devices, social computing) have on people's expectations for technology use in the enterprise.

Control plan A specific plan of action (including responsibilities and response to out-of-control conditions) that ensures that vital x's will be maintained at their optimal levels in order to optimize the process response (y).

Correlation The extent of an apparent relationship between two variables. Mathematically, correlation is indicated by r.

Critical to quality (CTQ) A characteristic or aspect of the product that is important to the customer/consumer.

Crowdsourcing The strategy of engaging wide internal audiences (i.e., sales teams) to contribute to the body of knowledge collected as part of the competitive intelligence strategy.

Customer relationship management (CRM)   A technology-enabled strategy for managing interactions with customers, clients, and prospects primarily around sales, marketing, customer service, and technical support activities.

Dashboard   A software-enabled capability to monitor key performance indicators (KPIs) related to a business process, often numerically and graphically oriented.

Define phase   The phase in Six Sigma quality improvement methodology where the goals and the scope of the improvement project are determined.

Democratization   A knowledge model in which all information originates from and is consumed by all stakeholders, and the organization serves to facilitate the distribution and governance of the information.

Disengaged   The state of an opportunity that has been placed on hold, where it is determined that there is no decision, or where the opportunity was deactivated before it was formally won or lost.

DMAIC   Acronym for the five major phases in the Six Sigma quality improvement methodology: *d*efine, *m*easure, *a*nalyze, *i*mprove, *c*ontrol.

Elicitation   Also referred to as "requirements gathering," this is the process of obtaining the requirements of a system from users, customers, and other stakeholders.

Executive sponsor   Typically, an executive or senior leader with a stake in the outcome of a project who supports the project team and helps to communicate project status within the organization.

Factor category   The general classification to which a specific factor belongs. Used to group factors for easier identification and selection.

Factor weighting   A numeric system used to assign the relative influences that selected factors have on the outcome of an opportunity.

Fishbone diagram   A visual tool used to organize the causes of a problem (the "effect"). Used to help identify root causes. Also known as a cause-and-effect diagram or Ishikawa diagram.

Forecast accuracy   The percentage variance over or under that actual sales compare with the forecasted amount. The time period is often stated on a monthly or quarterly basis.

Forensic sales   The discipline of examining the evidence of factors that led to a sales outcome and creating a new knowledge base from which to derive and apply the insights gained.

Hypothesis   A theory that is temporarily accepted in an attempt to explain certain conditions or to provide additional investigative guidance in order to interpret certain events or phenomena and to provide guidance for further investigation.

Improve phase   The phase of Six Sigma quality improvement methodology where current process methods are progressing toward the required level.

Institutionalize   To make standard operating procedure or policy across the entire organization.

Kano analysis   A quality measurement tool to help prioritize customer requirements (prioritized as dissatisfiers, satisfiers, and delighters).

Key performance indicators (KPIs)   Measurements taken on a near-real-time basis to track progress toward achieving program objectives.

Kotter model   A model developed by John Kotter in 1996 that specifies eight elements required to successfully manage change.

Loss   The outcome of an opportunity that was awarded to an opposing competitor.

Measure phase   The phase of Six Sigma quality improvement methodology where the performance of the current procedures or processes is documented.

Narrative   The supporting text entry describing or clarifying aspects of the opportunity.

Offering factors   Factors relating to the actual offering, such as product features, alignment with customer needs, price/value proposition, and strength of the solution.

Opportunity details   Objective attributes of a specific opportunity (e.g., deal amount, partners, competitors, location, etc.).

Opportunity outcome   The end stage of an active opportunity, typically classified as either a win or a loss. Other stages may exist (e.g., disengage, hold, etc.).

Outcome categories   The high-level groupings of the outcome factors; for example, "offering," "relationship," "competitive," and "services."

Outcome factor   Organized by category, these are the likely reasons that led to a particular outcome. Factors can be industry specific or can be broader in their definition.

Pocket BI   An emerging term that describes the delivery of business intelligence to portable devices, specifically mobile phones.

Postmortem   See "Win/loss review."

Primary factors   The factors that had the most influence on the final outcome of the opportunity, among the list of possible factors.

Process map   Typically found in process improvement disciplines such as Six Sigma, a problem-solving tool that graphically describes each step or phase in a process.

Relationship factors   The factors related to personal, team, or organizational relationship health.

Six Sigma   Six Sigma is the methodology developed by Motorola in the mid-1980s that provides businesses with the tools to improve the capability of their business processes.

SMART   Specific, measurable, attainable, relevant, time-bound—a simple mnemonic used during the project's objective-setting stage.

Social media Electronic media used for social interaction, typically Web-based and mobile technologies, to facilitate highly interactive communications.

Stakeholder Anyone who is affected by a project (or who can influence the project), but who is not necessarily involved in its implementation.

Stakeholder analysis A structured tool used to visually describe the current and desired states of stakeholder support for a project.

Tacit knowledge Knowledge primarily based on experience and observation that has not been formally documented or transmitted to others.

Voice of the customer (VoC) In the define phase of a Six Sigma project, the gathering of customer feedback, primarily through polling and surveys, that suggests broad and loosely defined needs of the customer. This feedback is then translated into critical to quality (CTQ).

Weighted factor A factor that carries a specific weighted value, allowing it to be compared in relative terms with other selected factors. The application of this methodology is useful when several factors are required to be selected, where each one is then ranked among the population.

Win The outcome of an opportunity that was awarded to the successful bidder or supplier.

Win/loss review The process by which the reasons for the deal outcome (i.e., won or lost) are reviewed, understood, and documented into a supporting platform or tool.

Win rate The calculated wins over all opportunities won, lost, or disengaged, over a given time period, often expressed as a function of opportunity count or opportunity revenue.

ABOUT THE AUTHOR

Rick Marcet has spent most of his 20-year professional career in marketing, technical sales, sales management, and sales operations in the high-tech software industry. His areas of expertise include driving enterprise sales performance, multidisciplinary sales models, and international business development. He is frequently invited to speak both within Microsoft Corporation and before industry associations and trade groups on topics related to sales excellence.

In his current role as Program Director for the World-Class Selling initiative at Microsoft Corporation, Rick leads the global program for transforming how sales managers coach high-performing sales teams, and how field sales teams optimize sales opportunities through a rigorous sales discipline balanced by both the art and science of selling.

His successes as an early practitioner of the field-generated win/loss review process gained him widespread recognition as a subject matter expert and an invitation by Microsoft's senior leadership to institutionalize and implement his award-winning methods on a global scale. The knowledge model developed to support these methods is reflected here in *Win/Loss Reviews.*

Rick graduated from Florida International University, majoring in International Business and Marketing, and is a certified Six Sigma Green Belt.

Rick lives in Bellevue, Washington, with his wife and two daughters. This is his first business title.

Contact information:

LinkedIn: www.linkedin.com/in/rickmarcet

Twitter: @rickmarcet

Facebook: facebook.com/pages/Win-Loss-Reviews/ 152317004835660

INDEX

Printed and bound by CPI Group (UK) Ltd, Croydon, CR0 4YY

16/04/2025